To Mary, for helping create this life
of startling delight.

Special Thanks to...

Terry Wardwell for sharing the fun of making Tuffits and the Web site,

Marjorie Baer and Cary Norsworthy for helping me get this book off the ground,

Nancy Davis, my editor and nerves-of-steel ground controller, for helping me land safely when the book was up in the air,

Nancy Aldrich-Ruenzel, Peachpit's publisher, for letting me fly in the first place,

David Van Ness and Lisa Brazieal for keeping the layouts and wing bolts tight,

Emily Glossbrenner for turning around the index faster than LAX does planes,

Laika for not eating all the free peanuts,

and my readers for fastening their safety belts during such extended metaphors.

contents

introduction   **vii**

what you'll create   viii   useful tools   xiii
how this book works   x   the next step   xiv
the web site   xii

1. welcome to dreamweaver   **1**

explore dreamweaver   2   extra bits   8
set up local site   4

2. create a basic home page   **9**

create your home page   10   create lists   18
add text   12   change the background 20
create headings   16   extra bits   22

3. add images   **23**

image tools   24   reduce image   30
add image   25   wrap text with images 32
crop image   27   align text with image 34
adjust brightness   29   extra bits   35

4. add tables   **37**

add a table   38   edit table   48
add image to table   40   format table colors   50
add labels   42   sort tables   51
save and apply style   44   extra bits   53
import tabular data   46

contents

5. create links   55

link text internally	56	add anchor link	65
link text externally	58	link image	67
color page links	59	create image map	68
color site links	60	extra bits	71
add email link	64		

6. reuse items to save time   73

create a favorite	74	create a template	82
create a library item	76	use your template	86
edit library item	78	edit template	89
insert library item	80	extra bits	91

7. add navigation   93

add layers	94	create main nav-bar	101
name layers	97	create small nav-bar	104
position layers	98	extra bits	110

8. publish site   111

add search terms	112	upload multiple files	120
check and fix links	114	upload a single page	122
explore the files panel	116	extra bits	123
connect to remote site	118		

index   125

introduction

The Visual QuickProject Guide that you hold in your hands offers a unique way to learn about new technologies. Instead of drowning you in theoretical possibilities and lengthy explanations, this Visual QuickProject Guide uses big, color illustrations coupled with clear, concise step-by-step instructions to show you how to complete one specific project in a matter of hours.

Our project in this book is to create a beautiful Web site using Macromedia Dreamweaver MX 2004, one of the best programs for building Web sites. Our Web site displays the products for a real company that makes cast concrete stepping stones that look like couch pillows. Because the project covers all the techniques needed to build a basic Web site, you'll be able to use what you learn to create your own Web site. Thanks to Dreamweaver, you'll do all this without having to enter a single line of HTML, the code that drives the Web.

what you'll create

These two pages represent just some of the things you'll learn how to create.

Format text and headings in the font, size, and colors you want. (See page 12.)

Add images and wrap text around them. (See page 23.)

Create a site-wide navigation bar to guide visitors as they explore your site. (See page 93.)

Reduce and resample images to make them quicker to download. (See page 30.)

Create internal, external, and email links, then give them a consistent appearance using external style sheets. (See page 55.)

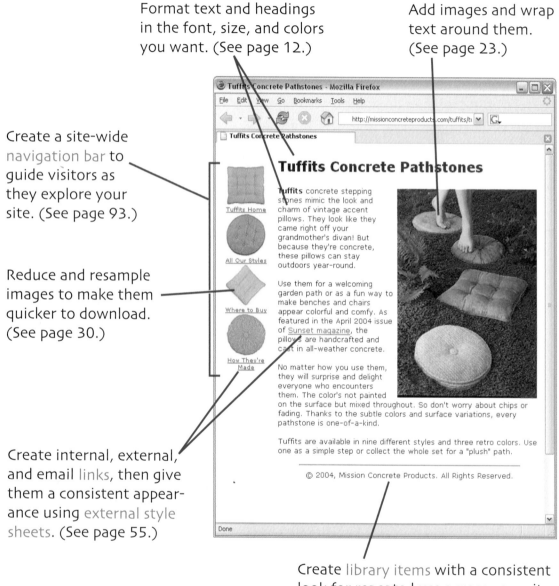

Create library items with a consistent look for repeated use across your site. (See page 76.)

Build tables for displaying everything from images to tabular data. (See page 37.)

Create image maps that link specific parts of images to different files. (See page 68.)

Apply colors and formatting to tables to make them easier to read. (See page 50.)

Sort data alphabetically or numerically within a table's columns or rows. (See page 51.)

Create anchor links so readers can jump to the right spot in a long document. (See page 65.)

Where to Buy Tuffits - Mozilla Firefox

File   Edit   View   Go   Bookmarks   Tools   Help

http://missionconcreteproducts.com/tuffits/tu

Where to Buy Tuffits

Where to Find Tuffits Near Your Home

California Retailers for Tuffits: Central, Bay Area, Northern, Southern

Central California

Retailer	Address	City	Zip	Phone
Air-Vol	P.O.Box 931	San Luis Obispo	93406	
Dinuba Garden Center	388 S.Alta	Dinuba	93618	
Peter Bros. Nursery	1135 S. GranadaDr.	Madera	93637	
Fresno Ag Hardware	4550 Blackstone Ave.	Fresno	93726	
Granite Rock Salinas	400 Work St.	Salinas	93901	
Hollister Landscape Supply		Hollister	93907	
Granite Rock Monterey	1755 Del Monte Blvd.	Monterey	93955	
H & H Home Center	P.O. Box 277	Seaside	93955	
Masonry Systems	3115 Railroad Ave..	Ceres	95307	

Bay Area

Retailer	Address	City	Zip
Half Moon Bay Bldg Material	119 Main St.	Half Moon Bay	94019
Los Altos Supply & Garden	4730 El Camino Real	Los Altos	94022

Done

how this book works

The title explains what is covered in that section.

Names of Dreamweaver elements, file names, and other important concepts are shown in orange.

Numbered steps lead you through the sequence of actions, showing only the details you really need.

Screenshots focus on what part of Dreamweaver you'll be using for that particular project step.

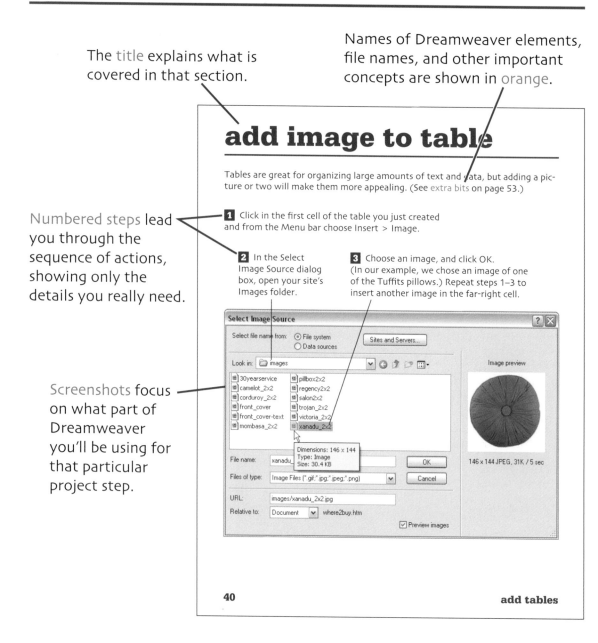

add image to table

Tables are great for organizing large amounts of text and data, but adding a picture or two will make them more appealing. (See extra bits on page 53.)

1 Click in the first cell of the table you just created and from the Menu bar choose Insert > Image.

2 In the Select Image Source dialog box, open your site's Images folder.

3 Choose an image, and click OK. (In our example, we chose an image of one of the Tuffits pillows.) Repeat steps 1–3 to insert another image in the far-right cell.

40

add tables

The extra bits section at the end of each chapter contains additional tips and tricks that you might like to know—but that aren't absolutely necessary for creating the Web page.

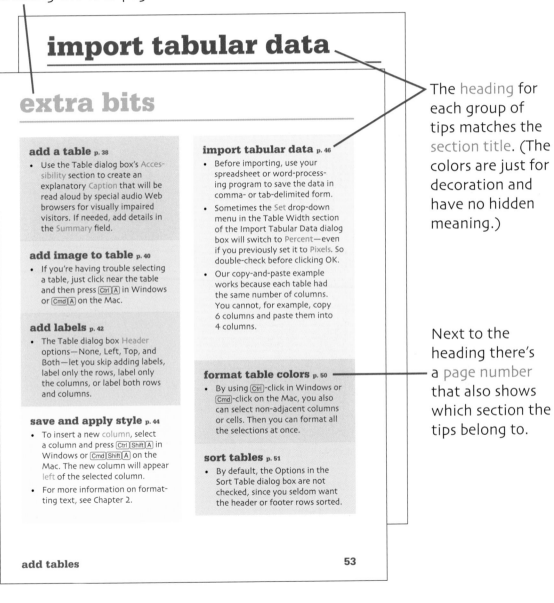

import tabular data

extra bits

add a table p. 38
- Use the Table dialog box's Accessibility section to create an explanatory Caption that will be read aloud by special audio Web browsers for visually impaired visitors. If needed, add details in the Summary field.

add image to table p. 40
- If you're having trouble selecting a table, just click near the table and then press Ctrl A in Windows or Cmd A on the Mac.

add labels p. 42
- The Table dialog box Header options—None, Left, Top, and Both—let you skip adding labels, label only the rows, label only the columns, or label both rows and columns.

save and apply style p. 44
- To insert a new column, select a column and press Ctrl Shift A in Windows or Cmd Shift A on the Mac. The new column will appear left of the selected column.
- For more information on formatting text, see Chapter 2.

import tabular data p. 46
- Before importing, use your spreadsheet or word-processing program to save the data in comma- or tab-delimited form.
- Sometimes the Set drop-down menu in the Table Width section of the Import Tabular Data dialog box will switch to Percent—even if you previously set it to Pixels. So double-check before clicking OK.
- Our copy-and-paste example works because each table had the same number of columns. You cannot, for example, copy 6 columns and paste them into 4 columns.

format table colors p. 50
- By using Ctrl-click in Windows or Cmd-click on the Mac, you also can select non-adjacent columns or cells. Then you can format all the selections at once.

sort tables p. 51
- By default, the Options in the Sort Table dialog box are not checked, since you seldom want the header or footer rows sorted.

add tables 53

The heading for each group of tips matches the section title. (The colors are just for decoration and have no hidden meaning.)

Next to the heading there's a page number that also shows which section the tips belong to.

the web site

You can find this book's companion site at http://www.waywest.net/dwvqj/.

You'll find all the example files used in the book, including the images.

You'll also find extra tips on working with Dreamweaver, plus corrections if any mistakes are found.

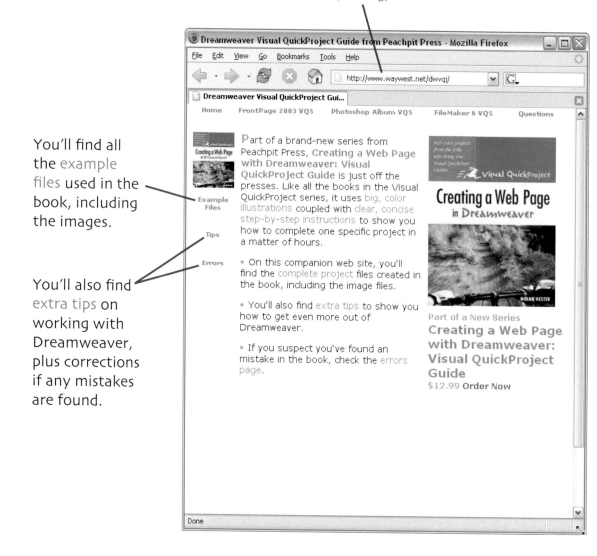

useful tools

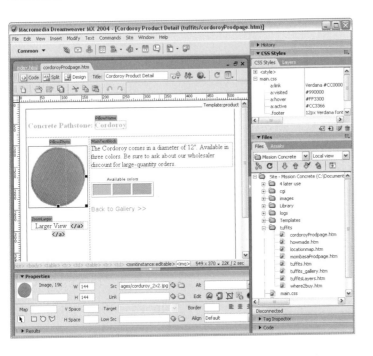

Naturally, you'll need a computer, and you'll need Dreamweaver MX 2004, which is packed with most of the tools you'll need, including a way to publish to the Web.

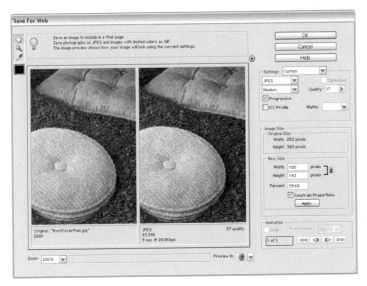

You'll also need an image editor. If you bought Dreamweaver as part of Macromedia Studio MX 2004, then you'll be able to use Fireworks, which is a full-fledged image editor designed to work hand-in-hand with Dreamweaver. Your digital camera may have included an image-editing program. Other-wise, consider Adobe Photoshop Elements, which also contains specific tools for working with Web images.

the next step

While this Visual QuickProject Guide gives you a good start on creating a Web site using Dreamweaver, there is a lot more to learn. If you want to dive into all the details, try Macromedia Dreamweaver MX 2004 for Windows and Macintosh: Visual QuickStart Guide, by J. Tarin Towers.

The Macromedia Dreamweaver MX 2004 Visual QuickStart Guide features clear examples, concise step-by-step instructions, and tons of helpful tips. With more than 700 pages, it covers darn near every aspect of Dreamweaver.

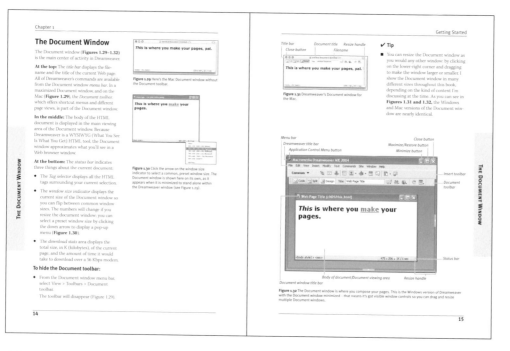

1. welcome to dreamweaver

Dreamweaver is a powerful program, packed with cool features to create Web sites. So packed, in fact, that it can be a bit overwhelming.

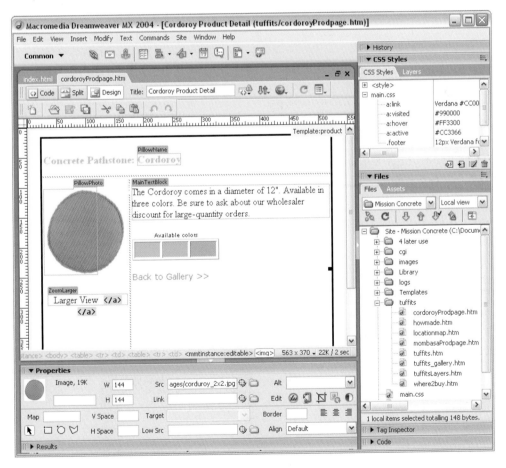

Not to worry. We aren't going to explain every possible option—just the crucial ones to keep you going, no matter how daunting Dreamweaver may seem initially. We'll have some fun along the way, too, so let's get started.

explore dreamweaver

A series of key toolbars, windows, and panels surround your main Dreamweaver document. Take a moment to understand how they work and you'll save yourself frustration later. (See extra bits on page 8.)

When you open more than one file, a series of tabs will appear across the top of the main window to indicate which ones are open.

The current file's title appears at the center of the toolbar, followed by some buttons related to posting your site on the Web. Use the last button if you want to see a ruler or grid while building pages.

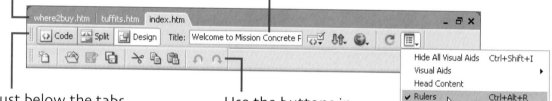

Just below the tabs run two toolbars. The Document toolbar is set by default to the Design view. You can change it to show only the Code view or use the Split view to show the Code and Design views.

Use the buttons in the Standard toolbar to create new files, open folders, cut and paste, save files, and undo actions.

Depending on what you're doing, switch the Insert toolbar to display the relevant buttons using the drop-down menu.

Many of the toolbar's buttons have their own drop-down menus.

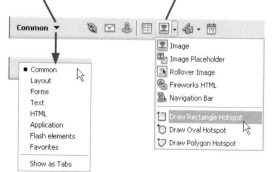

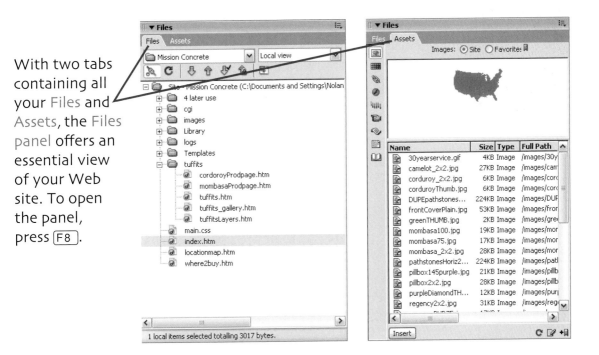

Depending on what you've selected, the Property inspector changes to display the relevant information and tools, such as those for text or images. To see or hide the inspector, press [Ctrl][F11] (Windows) or [Cmd][F11] (Mac).

With two tabs containing all your Files and Assets, the Files panel offers an essential view of your Web site. To open the panel, press [F8].

set up local site

Once you've installed Dreamweaver, your first step is to set up a local version of your Web site on your computer. (See extra bits on page 8.)

Macromedia Dreamweaver MX 2004

Open a Recent Item
- Open...

Create New
- HTML
- ColdFusion
- PHP
- ASP JavaScript
- ASP VBScript
- ASP.NET C#
- ASP.NET VB
- JSP
- CSS
- Dreamweaver Site...
- More...

Create from Samples
- CSS Style Sheets
- Framesets
- Page Designs (CSS)
- Page Designs
- Page Designs (Accessible)

Extend
- Dreamweaver Exchange

- Take a quick tour of Dreamweaver.
- Take a Dreamweaver tutorial.

Get the most out of Dreamweaver
Training, tips and tricks, special offers and more available at macromedia.com.

☐ Don't show again

1 Launch Dreamweaver and when the Start Page appears, click the Dreamweaver Site button.

welcome to dreamweaver

2 Dreamweaver will automatically assign a generic name to your new site and highlight it.

Site Definition for Unnamed Site 1

Basic | Advanced

Site Definition

Editing Files   Testing Files   Sharing Files

A site, in Macromedia Dreamweaver MX 2004, is a collection of files and folders that corresponds to a website on a server.

What would you like to name your site?

Unnamed Site 1

Example: mySite

3 Replace it with a more descriptive name. (In our example, it's Mission Concrete, the parent company of Tuffits Concrete Pathstones.)

If yo
serve
link c

Site Definition for Mission Concrete

Basic | Advanced

Site Definition

Editing Files   Testing Files   Sharing Files

A site, in Macromedia Dreamweaver MX 2004, is a collection of files and folders that corresponds to a website on a server.

What would you like to name your site?

Mission Concrete

Example: mySite

If you want to work directly on the server using FTP or RDS, you should create an FTP or RDS server connection instead. Server connections do not allow you to perform sitewide operations link checking or site reports.

< Back   Next >   Cancel   Help

4 Click Next to continue.

set up local site (cont.)

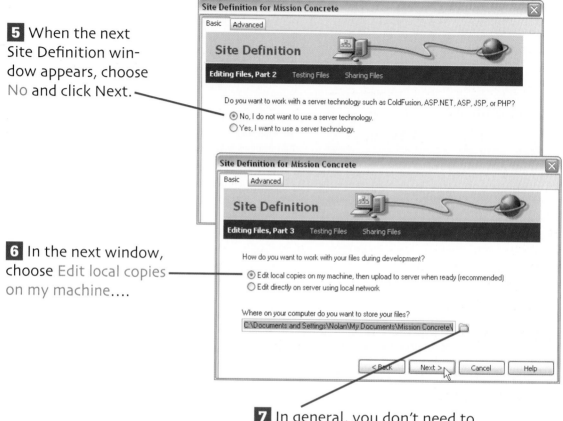

5 When the next Site Definition window appears, choose No and click Next.

6 In the next window, choose Edit local copies on my machine....

7 In general, you don't need to change where Dreamweaver creates the site folder, but if you want to change it, click the Folder icon and navigate to your preferred location. Click Next to continue.

welcome to dreamweaver

8 In the next window, choose FTP from the drop-down menu.

Fill in the FTP address for your new site, based on information provided by the firm that will be hosting your site.

Fill in your login and password, again based on the information from your Web host.

Assuming you're already online, click Test Connection and it will take only a moment for Dream-weaver to determine if the connection's working. Click Next to continue.

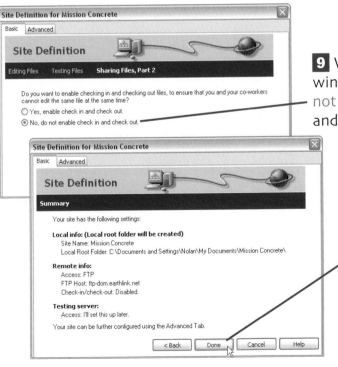

Site Definition for Mission Concrete

Basic | Advanced

Site Definition

Editing Files   Testing Files   **Sharing Files**

How do you connect to your remote server?
FTP

What is the hostname or FTP address of your Web server?
ftp-dom.earthlink.net

What folder on the server do you want to store your files in?

What is your FTP login:
www.missionconcreteproducts.com

What is your FTP password:
•••••••••••••••••••••••   ☑ Save

☐ Use Secure FTP (SFTP)

Test Connection

< Back   Next >   Cancel   Help

Site Definition for Mission Concrete

Basic | Advanced

Site Definition

Editing Files   Testing Files   **Sharing Files, Part 2**

Do you want to enable checking in and checking out files, to ensure that you and your co-workers cannot edit the same file at the same time?

○ Yes, enable check in and check out.
◉ No, do not enable check in and check out.

9 When the next Site Definition window appears, choose No, do not enable check in and check out and click Next.

Site Definition for Mission Concrete

Basic | Advanced

Site Definition

Summary

Your site has the following settings:

Local info: (Local root folder will be created)
   Site Name: Mission Concrete
   Local Root Folder: C:\Documents and Settings\Nolan\My Documents\Mission Concrete\

Remote info:
   Access: FTP
   FTP Host: ftp-dom.earthlink.net
   Check-in/check-out: Disabled.

Testing server:
   Access: I'll set this up later.

Your site can be further configured using the Advanced Tab.

< Back   Done   Cancel   Help

10 Double-check the Summary information before clicking Done. You're ready to build your site. See create a basic home page on page 9.

extra bits

explore dreamweaver p. 2

- Unless you're familiar with HTML or CSS coding, leave the toolbar set to Design.

- Rather than explain every tool and button here, we'll cover them in the coming chapters as we need them.

- You also can see or hide the contents of any panel by clicking the triangle-shaped arrow at the upper left of the panel.

- Using Dreamweaver's keyboard shortcuts greatly speeds your work.

  To download the Windows shortcuts, go to: http://download. macromedia.com/pub/dream weaver/documentation/dwmx_ kb_shortcuts.zip.

  To download the Mac shortcuts, go to: http://download.macro media.com/pub/dreamweaver/ documentation/dwmx_kb_ shortcuts.sit.

set up local site p. 4

- The name you enter in the Site Definition window only appears within Dreamweaver, not on your actual Web site. Pick one to distinguish this site from the many others you'll no doubt be creating soon.

- Web-hosting firms usually email you a login name and password for posting your files. Keep the original email where you won't delete it and can find it later. If you ever buy a new computer, you'll need that password because Dreamweaver never reveals the password, just those black dots.

- If the test connection fails, double-check your entries in the Site Definition window. Note that entries are case sensitive. Almost inevitably, you'll find a mistyped entry.

- Use the check-in system only if there are several people building the Web site; it keeps you from overwriting each other's work.

2. create a basic home page

As the front door to your Web site, the home page invites visitors to step in and take a look around. In this chapter, you'll build a simple home page to quickly orient visitors to what your site offers. In later chapters, you'll learn how to dress it up a bit with images and some special features. Here, however, we'll focus on the basics: creating, naming, titling, and saving this all-important page.

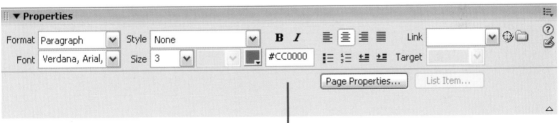

Working within Dreamweaver's Property inspector, you'll add text to the page, and set the font, size, color, and alignment. You'll also use the Property inspector to add headings and a bulleted list of items. Such lists help group multiple items into an easy-to-scan format. The graphics you add later will add snap to your Web pages, but such simple steps as formatting text and setting heading sizes establish an essential sense of order and visual rank on your pages.

create your home page

The mechanics of making your home page are pretty simple. The first step is to create a new page, then name the file, give it a title, and save it. While you can give the home page any title you wish, try to use something that helps visitors immediately understand your site's purpose. If you have not already done so, launch Dreamweaver, and the site you created in Chapter 1 will open by default. (See extra bits on page 22.)

From the Menu bar, choose File > New. When the New Document dialog box appears, under the General tab, select Basic page (HTML will be selected automatically) and click Create.

New Document

General | Templates

Category:
Basic page
Dynamic page
Template page
Other
CSS Style Sheets
Framesets
Page Designs (CSS)
Page Designs
Page Designs (Accessible)

Basic page:
HTML
HTML template
Library item
ActionScript
CSS
JavaScript
XML

Preview:

<No preview>

Description:
HTML document

☐ Make document XHTML compliant

Help | Preferences... | Get more content... | Create | Cancel

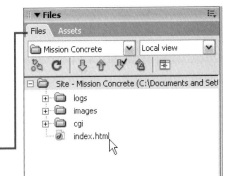

When a new untitled page appears in Dreamweaver's main window, click inside the Title text window, and type in your own title for the page. (Our sample site uses Welcome to Mission Concrete Products.) Visitors to your site will see the title at the top of their browser window, where it acts as a label for your site. It's not the same as the page's file name.

From the Menu bar, choose File > Save and in the Save As dialog box that opens, navigate to the site folder you created in Chapter 1. This will be your home page, so name it index and click Save. (Dreamweaver will automatically add the appropriate .htm or .html suffix.) The page will be saved and appear as part of your site in Dreamweaver's Files tab.

add text (cont.)

Continue to add lines and style text until you have all your information in place. Here we've added five more paragraphs of text, all using the centered black text of style1.

Stepping stones / Pavers / Edgers
Mortarless Building Block Systems
Landscape retaining-wall systems
Natural Stone
Tuffits decorative concrete pathstones

SERVING NORTHERN CALIFORNIA FOR MORE THAN 30 YEARS

▼ Properties

| Format | Paragraph | Style | style3 | **B** *I* | ≡ ≡ ≡ |
| Font | Default Font | Size | 12 | pixels | ≡ ≡ ≡ |

Page Prope

Press [Enter] (Windows) or [Return] (Mac) to create one last paragraph for a slogan, catchphrase, motto, or marketing message—something that quickly tells visitors what your site's all about and entices them to linger. We've used SERVING NORTHERN CALIFORNIA FOR MORE THAN 30 YEARS in all capital letters, selected the entire line, and chosen 12 in the Size drop-down menu.

That will make the text about 12 pixels high—just slightly smaller than the default 14 pixels that's applied when you set the Size drop-down menu to None. Notice that Dreamweaver saves this change as a new style, in this case style3 in the Style box.

Press [Enter] (Windows) or [Return] (Mac) to start a new
paragraph for your site's contact information. Type
Contact Us and then, because we want to present ──────┐
the rest of this information as a single item, press
[Shift] [←Enter] (Windows) or [Shift] [Return] (Mac) to create a simple line break. (Paragraph returns would
leave too much space between each line.)

Type the site's e-mail
address, and add more ───────
line breaks to place
the street address
and phone number
on separate lines of
their own.

Contact Us
gomcp@earthlink.net
125 N. 30th Street, San Jose CA 95116
(408) 998-2880

▼ **Properties**

Format	Paragraph	Style	style3	**B** *I*
Font	Default Font	Size	12	pixels

Now select the Contact Us line
and click the Bold icon in the ───────
Property inspector to highlight
this section. Save your changes
by choosing File > Save.

create a basic home page

create headings

Just like newspaper and magazine headlines, headings on a Web page are larger and more noticeable than regular text. They range from size 1 (the largest) to size 6 (the smallest). Use larger sizes for more important items and smaller sizes for less important items. (See extra bits on page 22.)

Select the first line of text in your home page (Mission Concrete Product in our sample project). In the Property inspector, select Heading 1 in the Format drop-down menu. The top line on the page will change from regular text to the larger, bolder Heading 1 style.

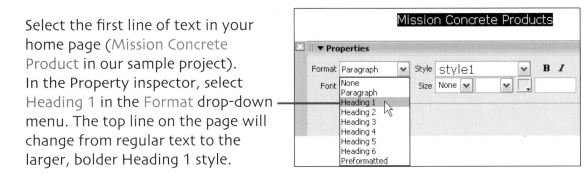

Select the second line (Concrete Landscape Products) and in the Property inspector, select Heading 3 in the Format drop-down menu. While the text will retain the red color last used for style2, its size and boldness change to reflect addition of the Heading 3 styling.

Mission Concrete Products

Concrete Landscape Products

Stepping stones / Pavers / Edgers
Mortarless Building Block Systems
Landscape retaining-wall systems
Natural Stone
Tuffits decorative concrete pathstones

▼ **Properties**

Format	Paragraph ▼	Style	style1 ▼	**B** *I*	≣ ≣ ≣ ≣	Link
Font	None	Size	None ▼	▼ ▢▾	⧉ ⧉ ⧉ ⧉	Target
	Paragraph					
	Heading 1				Page Properties...	
	Heading 2					
	Heading 3					
	Heading 4					
	Heading 5					
	Heading 6					
	Preformatted					

Click and drag your cursor to select the next five lines, which in our example lists various Mission Concrete products. In the Property inspector, select Heading 5 in the Format drop-down menu. All the lines change size, making it clearer that they are the items being referred to by the previous Concrete Landscape Products heading. To make that distinction even clearer, the next section shows how to format the products as a list. First, however, save your changes by choosing File > Save.

create a basic home page   **17**

create lists

Organizing information into lists, whether numbered or simply marked with bullets, makes it easy to group lots of items in a way that anyone can instantly recognize. Ordered lists are great when you need to highlight a specific sequence of steps or materials, but here we want to highlight the items without numbering them.

Return to your home page and select lines 3–7 on the home page. If it's not already visible, open the Property inspector (Window > Properties) and click the Ordered List icon, just above the Page Properties button.

▼ Properties

Format Heading 5   Style style1   **B** *I*

Font Verdana, Arial,   Size None

Page Properties.

Concrete Landscape Products

1. **Stepping stones / Pavers / Edgers**

2. **Mortarless Building Block Systems**

3. **Landscape retaining-wall systems**

4. **Natural Stone**

5. **Tuffits decorative concrete pathstones**

The selected lines will be numbered in sequence from 1 to 5 below the larger Concrete Landscape Products heading.

Reselect the five lines if they are no longer selected and click the Unordered List icon.

▼ Properties

Format | Heading 5 | Style | style1 | **B** *I*
Font | Verdana, Arial, | Size | None

Page Properties.

Concrete Landscape Products

- Stepping stones / Pavers / Edgers
- Mortarless Building Block Systems
- Landscape retaining-wall systems
  - Natural Stone
- Tuffits decorative concrete pathstones

The selected lines now will have small bullets instead, which in our example more clearly indicates that these are examples of Concrete Landscape Products. Save your changes by choosing File > Save.

change the background

You often see Web pages that use background images behind the text. Many of these pages use what's called a tiled image, where a small image is repeated across the page. Others use a single large image. In either case, unless the image is a very simple one, it can make it hard to read the page's text. Instead of adding an image, you can simply change the page's background from the default white to a color that makes your home page pop—without giving your visitors a headache.

Click the Page Properties button in the Property inspector.

In the Page Proper-
ties dialog box, click
the Background color's
drop-down menu and
pick a color that pro-
vides good contrast with
your text color. Click OK
to close the Page Prop-
erties dialog box.

create a basic home page

Mission Concrete Products

Concrete Landscape Products

- Stepping stones / Pavers / Edgers

- Mortarless Building Block Systems

- Landscape retaining-wall systems

- Natural Stone

- Tuffits decorative concrete pathstones

SERVING NORTHERN CALIFORNIA FOR MORE THAN 30 YEARS

Dreamweaver applies your changes to your home page. Save your changes by choosing from the Menu bar File > Save. In the next chapter, you'll learn how to add graphics to your pages to catch a visitor's attention—without interfering with the text's readability.

extra bits

create your home page p. 10

- The page's file name and title serve different purposes. The file name is used behind the scenes to help you and Dreamweaver keep track of how your files are organized. For example, home pages should always be named index, which helps Web servers know that this page is the "front door" to your site. The page title is what the viewer's Web browser displays when your page is onscreen.

- The Basic Page column offers lots of choices, including templates and library items. Both are explained in later chapters (see pages 76 and 82). Working with non-HTML pages, such as those using CSS and XML, is covered in the Dreamweaver MX 2004: Visual QuickStart Guide.

- If your options are set so the Start Page appears when Dreamweaver launches, you can create a new page by clicking HTML in the Create New column.

add text p. 12

- If you are building your Web site on a Windows PC, be kind to Mac-based visitors by not using the smallest text sizes. If you're creating pages with a Mac, remember that text columns should have enough space at the bottom to handle the text running about 25 percent longer when viewed on a Windows machine.

- While you can choose Edit Font List to pick a particular font installed on your own computer, there's no guarantee visitors will have the font, so stick to the six most common font groups.

- Dreamweaver automatically defines and saves your different type settings as separate styles, based on a system called Cascading Style Sheets (CSS). The information includes such things as the text's format, font, size, alignment, and color. Dreamweaver arbitrarily names your first text setting style 1. When you create or change that type setting—as you did by adding red to the second line of text—Dreamweaver saves the new style as style 2. While entire books are devoted to CSS, you don't need to know much more than such style sheets make it easy to reuse text styles without starting from scratch.

create headings p. 16

- To keep your pages uncluttered, limit yourself to no more than two or three heading sizes on the same page.

3. add images

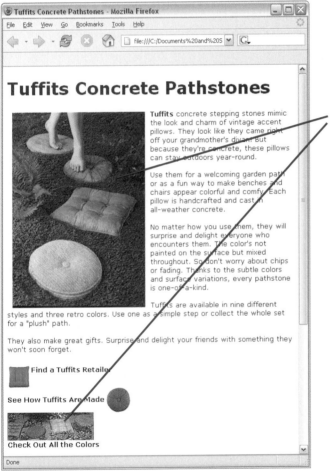

While text and headlines lend structure and meaning to Web pages, it's images that give them real impact.

Dreamweaver can handle basic image editing; for more demanding tasks use a dedicated graphics program. If you don't already have a graphics program, take a look in the graphics section of www.versiontracker.com where you can compare prices, features, and user comments.

image tools

As with text-related tasks, the Property inspector acts as your main tool for most image work.

Displayed near the image thumbnail is the file size (53K in our example) and its W (width) and H (height) in pixels.

Scr tells you where the image is stored, while Link tells you what file (if any) the image is linked to if clicked.

Alt lets you create a label to be read aloud by browsers created for visually handicapped visitors. Use Alt to describe an image for visitors who have turned off image downloading for speedier surfing.

▼ Properties									
	Image, 53K	W	252	Src	/frontCoverPlain.jpg		Alt	person steps on sto	
		H	360	Link			Edit		
Map		V Space	4	Target			Border		
	H Space	10	Low Src			Align	Left		

The items from Map to Target are used to create image maps, as explained on pages 68–70.

Three of the Edit buttons only work if you have installed Macromedia Fireworks. Without Fireworks, you're limited to using the Crop, Contrast/Brightness, and Sharpen buttons (see pages 27, 29, and 30).

Use Border to set the border width around the image. The three buttons to the right control whether your image is set at the left, center, or right of the page. Use the Align drop-down menu to control how text wraps around the image (see pages 32–34).

add image

After preparing images in an external program, you're ready to add them to your Web pages. (See extra bits on page 35.)

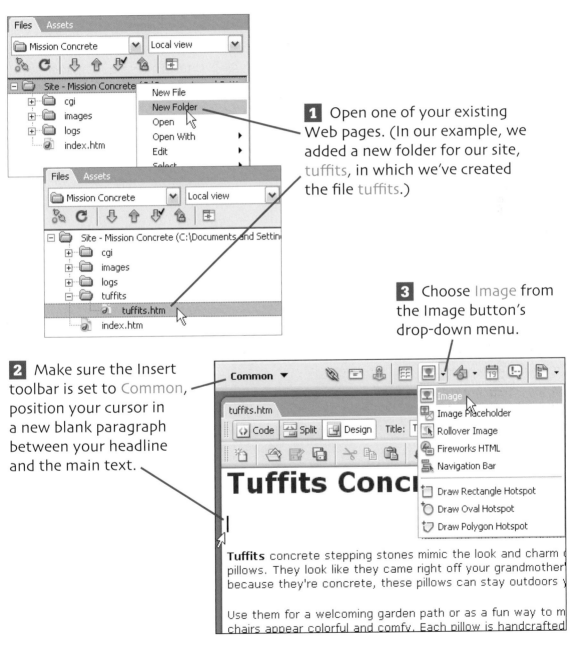

1 Open one of your existing Web pages. (In our example, we added a new folder for our site, tuffits, in which we've created the file tuffits.)

3 Choose Image from the Image button's drop-down menu.

2 Make sure the Insert toolbar is set to Common, position your cursor in a new blank paragraph between your headline and the main text.

add image (cont.)

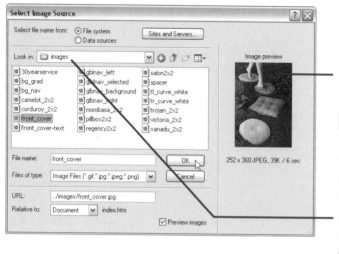

4 When the Select Image Source dialog box appears, navigate to the image you want to use (using the preview area to help you choose), and click OK.

5 If the image isn't already a part of your Web site, Dreamweaver will ask if you want to save it in the site's root folder. Choose Yes, navigate to your site's images, and save the image there. The selected image will appear between the headline and the main text.

6 Once inserted on the page, the image remains selected, so click the align center button in the Property inspector to center the image on the page.

7 Type a brief description of the image in the Alt text box. Save the page before continuing.

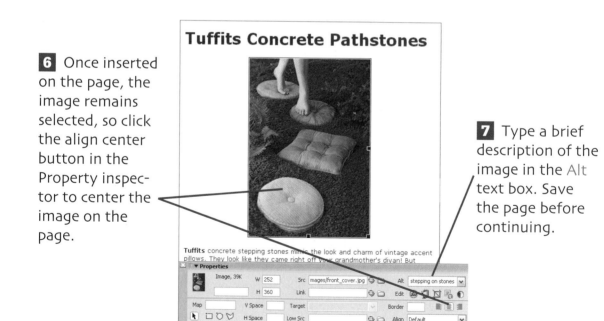

crop image

You don't need a separate graphics program for cropping images—just don't use your original image. Cropping permanently alters your image, so if you make a mistake, immediately choose Undo Crop in the Edit menu. (See extra bits on page 35.)

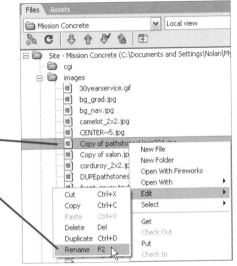

Select the original image in your site's Files panel and duplicate it (Ctrl D in Windows, Cmd D on the Mac). Dreamweaver auto-matically adds Copy of to beginning of the duplicate's file name.

If you want to name it something else, right-click (Windows) or Ctrl-click (Mac) it and choose Rename from the Edit drop-down menu. Once the name is highlighted, type in a new name and press Enter (Windows) or Return (Mac).

Insert the image on the page and select it by clicking on it. Make sure the Property inspector is visible and click the Crop button in the Prop-erty inspector. A selection area, marked by a dashed line and darker surrounding area, will appear in the middle of the image.

crop image (cont.)

Click and drag any of the black handles along the selection's edge to set your crop lines or click-and-drag in the middle to reposition the entire crop.

Double-click inside the selection and the image will be trimmed.

adjust brightness

A single button in the Property inspector lets you adjust an image's brightness or contrast. Sometimes minor adjustments of either can really help a so-so image. You do not need to make a duplicate of the image. (See extra bits on page 35.)

Click to select the image on your page that you want to adjust.

Now click the Brightness and Contrast button in the Property inspector.

To change the brightness or contrast drag the sliders or enter new values in the adjacent text windows. (Increase the effects by sliding to the right or entering a larger number.) Click OK to apply your adjustments.

reduce image

If you have an image without lots of details, which would disappear if shrunk, you can use it to create a tiny thumbnail to add some graphic variety to a page. Detail lost from reducing and resampling cannot be recovered, so use a duplicate of your original image. (See extra bits on page 35.)

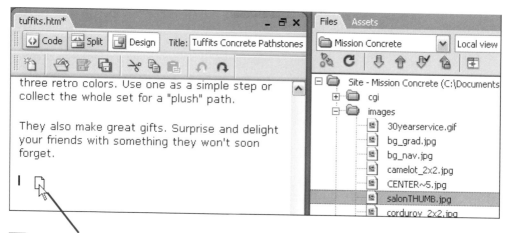

1 Make a duplicate of your original image, and drag the renamed image—salonTHUMB.jpg in our example—onto the page. The image will appear on the page with small black handles at its corners.

2 Press [Shift] while dragging a corner handle to reduce the image yet maintain its proportions.

Watch the pixel dimensions change in the W and H text windows in the Property inspector to gauge how much to reduce the image.

Image, 19K   W 45   H 42

3 Release the cursor and the image will appear with the new dimensions in bold—even though the actual size of the file remains the same.

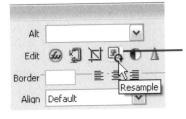

4 Click the Property inspector's Resample button to reduce the actual file size, indicated afterward by a smaller K size in the Property inspector.

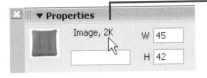

5 Greatly reduced images often lose some crispness, so click the Sharpen button.

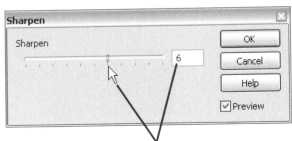

6 Use the slider or text window in the Sharpen dialog box to adjust the amount. (Drag slider to the right or enter a higher number in the text window to increase the sharpening.) Click OK when you're satisfied. Save the page before continuing.

add images

wrap text with images

Wrapping blocks of text around your images, instead of putting each image in its own paragraph, creates a tighter, more professional page layout. (See extra bits on page 35.)

Tuffits concrete
the look and charm of vintage accent pillows. They look
off your grandmother's divan! But because they're conc
can stay outdoors year-round.

Use them for a welcoming garden path or as a fun way
chairs appear colorful and comfy. Each pillow is handcra
weather concrete.

1 Click at the beginning of the text paragraph and press ←Backspace (Windows) or Delete (Mac) once to remove the paragraph break separating the image from the text below it.

Tuffits concrete stepping stones mimic
the look and charm of vintage accent
pillows. They look like they came right
off your grandmother's divan! But
because they're concrete, these
pillows can stay outdoors year-round.

Use them for a welcoming garden path
or as a fun way to make benches and
chairs appear colorful and comfy. Each
pillow is handcrafted and cast in all-
weather concrete.

No matter how you use them, they will
surprise and delight everyone who
encounters them. The color's not
painted on the surface but mixed
throughout. So don't worry about
chips or fading. Thanks to the subtle
colors and surface variations, every
pathstone is one-of-a-kind.

Tuffits are available in nine different
styles and three retro colors. Use one as a simple step or collect the whole
set for a "plush" path.

2 Select the image and use the Align drop-down menu to choose Left. The image will be aligned on the left side of the page with the text wrapping along its right side.

▼ Properties

	Image, 39K	W	252	Src	mages/front_cover.jpg		Alt	stepping on stones
		H	360	Link			Edit	
Map		V Space		Target			Border	
		H Space		Low Src			Align	Left

add images

3 To add a little more space between the image and the surrounding text, make sure the image is selected. Now use the H Space text box to specify how many pixels of space you want between the image and text. In our example, we set the H at 10, which adds a moderate amount of space.

pathstone is one-of-a-kind.

Tuffits
mimic t
vintage
like the
grandm
they're
can sta

Use the
path or
benche
and cor
handcra
weathe

No mat
they wi
everyor
The col
surface
don't w
Thanks
surface

▼ Properties
Image, 53K   W 252   Src ies/fro
H 360   Link
Map   V Space   Target
H Space 10   Low Src

everyone w
The color's
surface but
don't worry
Thanks to t
surface var
pathstone i

Tuffits are available in nine different styles and three

▼ Properties
Image, 53K   W 252   Src ies/frontCov
H 360   Link
Map   V Space 10   Target
H Space 10   Low Src

4 Use the V Space text box to set how many pixels are added above and below the image, which affects how closely the text wraps under the image. Save the page before continuing.

surface bu
don't worry
Thanks to t
surface var

pathstone is one-of-a-kind.

Tuffits are available in nine different styles and three

▼ Properties
Image, 53K   W 252   Src ies/frontCov
H 360   Link
Map   V Space 2   Target
H Space 10   Low Src

add images

align text with image

The same Align drop-down menu used to wrap blocks of text around images also can be used to precisely position an image next to a single line of text. It's especially useful for pairing button-sized images with text labels.

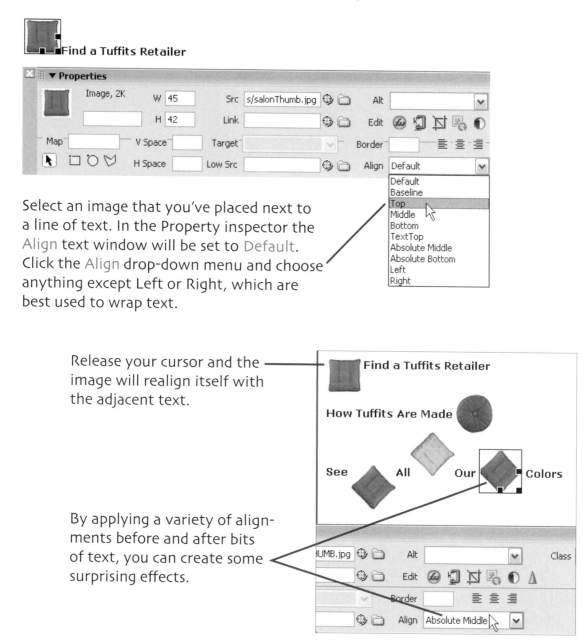

Find a Tuffits Retailer

Select an image that you've placed next to a line of text. In the Property inspector the Align text window will be set to Default. Click the Align drop-down menu and choose anything except Left or Right, which are best used to wrap text.

Release your cursor and the image will realign itself with the adjacent text.

By applying a variety of alignments before and after bits of text, you can create some surprising effects.

extra bits

image tools p. 24

- The blank text window right of the thumbnail is for scripts.

add image p. 25

- Keep your site's top-level folder uncluttered by creating new subfolders when you have more than three or four related pages. Open the Files panel and right-click (Windows) or Option-click (Mac) to reveal the New Folder choice.

- The root folder contains all your Web site's files. (In our example, it's Mission Concrete.) Save photos/graphics to the auto-generated subfolder, images, to easily find them.

- Listed below the image preview are its dimensions, file size, and estimated download time.

- Always add Alt text for your images. For dialup Web visitors, the alt text appears quickly, enabling them to skip the page if they don't want to wait for the full image. Alt text also is used by special audio Web browsers for visually impaired visitors. If the image is something like a horizontal rule, choose < empty > from the drop-down menu.

crop image p. 27

- Dreamweaver's built-in image editing only works for JPEG and GIF images, the two formats used for most photos and graphics.

adjust brightness p. 29

- The sliders can be hard to control, so type numbers in the text windows for fine adjustments.

reduce image p. 30

- You could use resampling to enlarge an image, but don't. The quality will suffer noticeably. Instead, use your regular image-editing program with the (presumably) larger original.

- When you click the Resample button, a dialog box warns you that the change is permanent. Since we're using a duplicate, click OK.

wrap text with images p. 32

- To put the image on the right side with the text down the left, choose Right in the Property inspector's Align drop-down menu.

- The Property inspector's H Space and V Space values are added to both sides of the image (right and left, top and bottom).

4. add tables

You are not limited to the simple approach used to build your home page in Chapter 2. By using tables to lay out a page, you can create pages more quickly and consistently. Tables also allow you to mix text, data, images, and headers, yet present it all in an easy to organize manner.

Where to Buy Tuffits

Where to Find Tuffits Near Your Home

California Retailers for Tuffits

Retailer	Address	City	Zip
Big B Lumber	6600 Brentwood Blvd..	Brentwood	94513
Norman's Brentwood Nursery	Route 3 Box 526	Brentwood	94513
Masonry Systems	3115 Railroad Ave..	Ceres	95307
L.H.Voss	2445 Vista Del Monte.	Concord	94520
Yamagami's Nursery	1361 South DeAnza Blvd.	Cupertino	95014
Dinuba Garden Center	388 S.Alta	Dinuba	93618
Agorra Bldg Supply	5965 Dougherty Road	Dublin	94568
Christy Vault Co.	44100 Christy St.	Fremont	94538
Regan Nursery.Inc.	4268 Decoto Rd.	Fremont	94555
Fresno Ag Hardware	4550 Blackstone Ave.	Fresno	93726

add a table

Tables can be a big help in creating simple layouts for your pages. (See extra bits on page 53.)

1 As you did in the previous chapter, create a new basic Web page (Ctrl N in Windows, Cmd N on the Mac) and give it a title by typing inside the Title text window.

2 Save it before continuing (Ctrl S in Windows, Cmd S on the Mac). (In our example, we titled the new page Where to Buy Tuffits and saved the file as where2buy.)

Take a moment to set several Dreamweaver options that will make using tables easier.

3 Set the Insert toolbar to Layout.

4 And click the Standard button near the center of the toolbar...

...which will display buttons for inserting tables and columns.

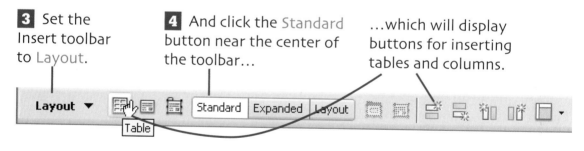

5 To make it easier to align your tables and cells, turn on the ruler (View > Rulers > Show), the grid (View > Grid > Show Grid), and set the grid so your drawn objects snap to it (View > Grid > Snap To Grid).

add tables

6 Click inside your page, then click the Insert Table button in the Layout toolbar. When the Table dialog box appears, use the text boxes to set the Table size and whether you want a Header, which lets you create labels for your rows or columns. In our example, we've set Rows to 1, Columns to 3, Table width to 500 pixels, Border thickness to 1 pixel, and the Header to None. Click OK to insert the new table.

Table

Table size

Rows: 1   Columns: 3
Table width: 500   pixels ▼
Border thickness: 1   pixels
Cell padding:
Cell spacing:

Header

None   Left   Top   Both

Accessibility

Caption:
Align caption: top ▼
Summary:

Help   OK   Cancel

Where to Find Tuffits Near Your Home

500 ▼

7 When the new table appears, click inside the middle cell to type a headline for the page. (Our example includes a line break right after Tuffits.) Based on what you learned in Chapter 2, use the Property inspector to format the cell's text.

add image to table

Tables are great for organizing large amounts of text and data, but adding a picture or two will make them more appealing. (See extra bits on page 53.)

1 Click in the first cell of the table you just created and from the Menu bar choose Insert > Image.

2 In the Select Image Source dialog box, open your site's Images folder.

3 Choose an image, and click OK. (In our example, we chose an image of one of the Tuffits pillows.) Repeat steps 1–3 to insert another image in the far-right cell.

Select Image Source

Select file name from: ⦿ File system ○ Data sources   [Sites and Servers...]

Look in: 📁 images

30yearservice	pillbox2x2
camelot_2x2	regency2x2
corduroy_2x2	salon2x2
front_cover	trojan_2x2
front_cover-text	victoria_2x2
mombasa_2x2	xanadu_2x2

Dimensions: 146 x 144
Type: Image
Size: 30.4 KB

File name: xanadu_   [OK]

Files of type: Image Files (*.gif;*.jpg;*.jpeg;*.png)   [Cancel]

URL: images/xanadu_2x2.jpg

Relative to: Document ▾ where2buy.htm

☑ Preview images

Image preview

146 x 144 JPEG, 31K / 5 sec

567

4 Even though the table has automatically expanded to 567 pixels, the two pillow images have squeezed the middle cell so that the text now requires four lines. To widen the table enough for two text lines, click the table's corner and drag the corner handle to 600 pixels.

5 Press ⇧Shift⏎Enter (Windows) or ⇧Shift⏎Return (Mac) to start a new line, then insert a horizontal rule to set off this table from the rest of the page by choosing Insert > HTML > Horizontal Rule. Use the Property inspector to place the rule to the Left and make it 2 pixels high.

▼ Properties						
	Horizontal rule	W	600	pixels	Align	Left
		H	2			Default
						Left
						Center
						Right

add labels

Dreamweaver automatically formats row and column labels as centered and bold. That makes the labels, also known as table headers, easy to scan for anyone viewing the table. (See extra bits on page 53.)

Press [Enter] (Windows) or [Return] (Mac) to start a new line below the first table, then insert a new table and use the Table dialog box to set the Table size, and create a Header with labels across the Top.

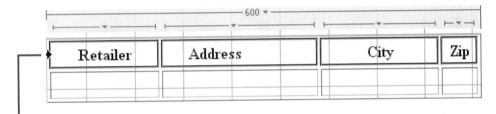

When the new table appears on the page, click in the header's far-left cell and type in a label for the first column. Add labels for the rest of the headers, pressing [Tab] to move from cell to cell. (In our example, we use Retailer, Address, City, and Zip, which match the tabular data we'll soon import.)

Select the header row by moving your cursor to the row's left edge until it becomes a bold arrow and the selected row is outlined in red. With the row selected, use the Property inspector to change the font and size and press [Tab] to apply the changes to all the text in the row.

add tables

save and apply style

By saving and renaming the CSS-based styles that Dreamweaver automatically generates as you change text settings, you can reapply those same settings later to other text selections. (See extra bits on page 53.)

In our table header example, the Font is set to Verdana, Arial, Helvetica, san-serif, the Size at 12 in Bold, with a light-gray Bg (background color) of #CCCCCC. By default, Dreamweaver automatically generated a temporary name of style12 for all these changes.

Since we want to apply this same style for other table headers, we'll give it an easy to recognize permanent name. Click the Style dropdown menu and choose Rename.

When the Rename Style dialog box appears, type a quick descriptive name in the New name text box (no spaces allowed) and click OK to save the new name. The new name will appear in the Property inspector's Style text box.

Now, let's apply the style to a new row inserted just above the header row. Select the header, and press Ctrl M in Windows or Cmd M on the Mac to insert the row.

In our example, the new row has four cells, just like the row below it. To merge them into a single cell, select the new row and press Ctrl Alt M in Windows or Cmd Option M on the Mac.

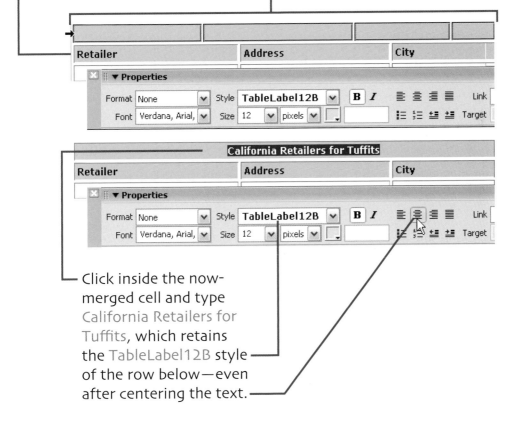

Click inside the now-merged cell and type California Retailers for Tuffits, which retains the TableLabel12B style of the row below—even after centering the text.

import tabular data

Nothing beats a table for clearly presenting spreadsheet data or tab-separated text imported from a word-processing document. (See extra bits on page 53.)

1 Press [Enter] (Windows) or [Return] (Mac) to start a new paragraph just below the table you've already created.

2 Click the Tabular Data icon in the Layout toolbar to open the Import Tabular Data dialog box.

3 Click Browse to navigate to where you've stored the spreadsheet or word-processing document.

4 For the Delimiter use Tab (or whatever you used in the document you're importing), in the Table width section choose Set and use the adjacent text windows to specify that width, skip the padding and spacing settings, set the Format top row to [No Formatting] and click OK.

California Retailers for Tuffits			
Retailer	Address	City	Zip
600 ▼			
▼	▼	▼	▼
Agorra Bldg Supply	5965 Dougherty Road	Dublin	94568
Clark's Home and Garden	23040 Clawiter Rd.	Hayward	94545
Christv Vault Co.	44100 Christy St.	Fremont	94538
Diamond K Supply	3671 Mt.Diablo Blvd.	Lafayette	94549
L.H.Voss	2445 Vista Del Monte.Concord	94520	
Morgan's Masonry	P.O. Box 127	San Ramon	94583

5 The data will appear on the Web page arranged in its own table. Save the page (Ctrl S in Windows, Cmd S on the Mac).

6 Click and drag your cursor until you select all the cells in the second table, then copy them (press Ctrl C in Windows, Cmd C on the Mac).

Agorra Bldg Supply	5965 Dougherty Road	Dublin
Clark's Home and Garden	23040 Clawiter Rd.	Hayward
Christv Vault Co.	44100 Christy St.	Fremont
Diamond K Supply	3671 Mt.Diablo Blvd.	Lafayette
L.H.Voss	2445 Vista Del Monte.Concord	94520
Morgan's Masonry	P.O. Box 127	San Ram
Morgan Bros. Patio	14305 Washington Ave.	San Lean

mino Real	Los Altos	94022
Blvd.	Redwood City	94062
lyn Ave.	Mountain View	94041
t.	Mountain View	94041
re Blvd.	San Francisco	94124
Ave.	Sunnyvale	94086
lway	Vallejo	94591

7 Click in the first cell in the blank row of the top table and paste your selection there (press Ctrl V in Windows, Cmd V on the Mac). The copied cells will appear in the first table with their cell formatting intact. Having moved the second table's contents to the first table, select the second table and delete it.

California Retailers for Tuffits			
Retailer	Address	City	Zip
Agorra Bldg Supply	5965 Dougherty Road	Dublin	94568
Clark's Home and Garden	23040 Clawiter Rd.	Hayward	94545
Christv Vault Co.	44100 Christy St.	Fremont	94538
Diamond K Supply	3671 Mt.Diablo Blvd.	Lafayette	94549
L.H.Voss	2445 Vista Del Monte.Concord	94520	
Morgan's Masonry	P.O. Box 127	San Ramon	94583
Morgan Bros. Patio	14305 Washington Ave.	San Leandro	94578
Orco Const. Supply	P.O. Box5058	Livermore	94550

add tables

edit table

Inevitably, our example table has a few errors. Several blank cells appear because the imported data mistakenly had an extra tab character between several retailers' names and addresses. Dreamweaver makes it easy to fix the problem, but let's first change the new table text formatting.

1 Click and drag your cursor to select all the text cells in the table and use the Property inspector to set the Font, Size, and cell alignment.

2 Press Tab to apply the formatting and to trigger Dreamweaver to generate a generic name for your new style. (In our example, Dreamweaver named it style35.) Use the Style drop-down menu to rename it something easy to remember for reuse. (In our example, we will name it TableText10 since we want to reuse the 10-pixel style in future tables.)

add tables

3 You cannot directly delete a blank cell in a table because of the table's interlocking grid of rows and columns. But you can move data from several cells and delete the blank row created by the shift. (In our example, we select the cell with the street address for the first retailer.)

Broadmoor Lumber Co.		1350 El Camino Real	S.S.F.
94080			

Broadmoor Lumber Co.	1350 El Camino Real		S.S.F.
94080			

Broadmoor Lumber Co.	1350 El Camino Real	S.S.F.	94080

4 Click and drag to select the text, then drag the highlighted text from one cell to the other.

5 Repeat for the misplaced city and zip code data, which will leave you a blank row that you can select and delete.

add tables

format table colors

To make it easier for your Web visitors to read the information in long tables, we'll apply some color formatting. (See extra bits on page 53.)

Select the entire table and choose Commands > Format Table to open the Format Table dialog box, which includes more than a dozen preset table color combinations.

Use the various drop-down menus to pick your colors and how often the colors of the rows alternate.

In our example, we've changed the First and Second row colors to echo the page's pillow colors and set Alternate to Every Two Rows for a less busy look.

Click Apply to preview your choices and click OK to close the dialog box. Be sure to save the page when you're done.

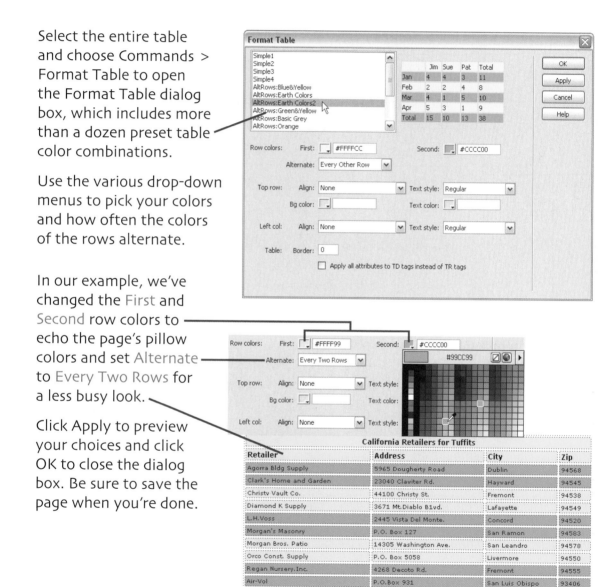

sort tables

Dreamweaver can automatically sort tabular data by column—a neat trick that lets you tinker with how the data is organized long after you've imported it into your table. There's just one catch: tables cannot be sorted if they include a cell that spans multiple columns. We've got just such a cell in our example, but we can do a quick cut and paste to work around this restriction. (See extra bits on page 53.)

Select the column-spanning cell (in our example, it's California Retailers for Tuffits) and cut it from the page (Ctrl X in Windows, Cmd X on the Mac). Now select the table and choose Commands > Sort Table to open the Sort Table dialog box.

Use the Sort by drop-down menu to choose which column will control the sort, then use the Order drop-down menu to set whether the sort is done Alphabetically (or numerically) and whether it's Ascending (or descending) order. (In our example, we sort by Column 3 (City) because that will be the easiest way for site visitors to find a nearby store. We also set Then by to sort using Column 4 (Zip), which will help big-city residents. Click Apply to preview the sort and click OK to close the dialog box.

Address	City	Zip
6600 Brentwood Blvd..	Brentwood	94513
Route 3 Box 526	Brentwood	94513
3115 Railroad Ave..	Ceres	95307
2445 Vista Del Monte.	Concord	94520
1361 South DeAnza Blvd.	Cupertino	95014
388 S.Alta	Dinuba	93618
5965 Dougherty Road	Dublin	94568
44100 Christy St.	Fremont	94538
4268 Decoto Rd.	Fremont	94555
4550 Blackstone Ave.	Fresno	93726
6475 Chesnut	Gilroy	95020
281 Yamane Dr.	Gilroy	95020

sort tables (cont.)

Once the sort's done, insert a row above the header row, merge those new cells into one and paste back in your original header. (In our example, it's California Retailers for Tuffits.) Be sure to save the page and you're done.

California Retailers for Tuffits			
Retailer	**Address**	**City**	**Zip**
Big B Lumber	6600 Brentwood Blvd..	Brentwood	94513
Norman's Brentwood Nursery	Route 3 Box 526	Brentwood	94513
Masonry Systems	3115 Railroad Ave..	Ceres	95307

extra bits

add a table p. 38

- Use the Table dialog box's Accessibility section to create an explanatory Caption that will be read aloud by special audio Web browsers for visually impaired visitors. If needed, add details in the Summary field.

add image to table p. 40

- If you're having trouble selecting a table, just click near the table and then press Ctrl A in Windows or Cmd A on the Mac.

add labels p. 42

- The Table dialog box Header options—None, Left, Top, and Both—let you skip adding labels, label only the rows, label only the columns, or label both rows and columns.

save and apply style p. 44

- To insert a new column, select a column and press Ctrl Shift A in Windows or Cmd Shift A on the Mac. The new column will appear left of the selected column.
- For more information on formatting text, see Chapter 2.

import tabular data p. 46

- Before importing, use your spreadsheet or word-processing program to save the data in comma- or tab-delimited form.
- Sometimes the Set drop-down menu in the Table Width section of the Import Tabular Data dialog box will switch to Percent—even if you previously set it to Pixels. So double-check before clicking OK.
- Our copy-and-paste example works because each table had the same number of columns. You cannot, for example, copy 6 columns and paste them into 4 columns.

format table colors p. 50

- By using Ctrl-click in Windows or Cmd-click on the Mac, you also can select non-adjacent columns or cells. Then you can format all the selections at once.

sort tables p. 51

- By default, the Options in the Sort Table dialog box are not checked, since you seldom want the header or footer rows sorted.

5. create links

The Web's magic comes largely from the hyperlink, which lets Web users jump from page to image to email to almost anywhere on the Internet. Links fall into two categories: internal links, which connect different items within your own Web site, and external links, which connect to items out on the larger Web. Before we begin linking some of the pages created in previous chapters, switch the Insert toolbar to Common, which includes link-related buttons.

Add link   Add anchor link

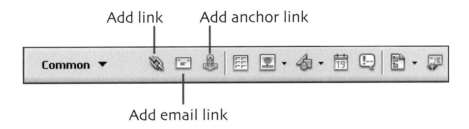

Add email link

link text internally

Dreamweaver makes creating links between pages on your Web site a point-and-click affair. (See extra bits on page 71.)

1 Open your home page and select text you want to link to another page on your Web site. (In our example, we are linking text on the Mission Concrete home page to the Tuffits products page.)

2 Make sure the Files panel and the Property inspector are both visible.

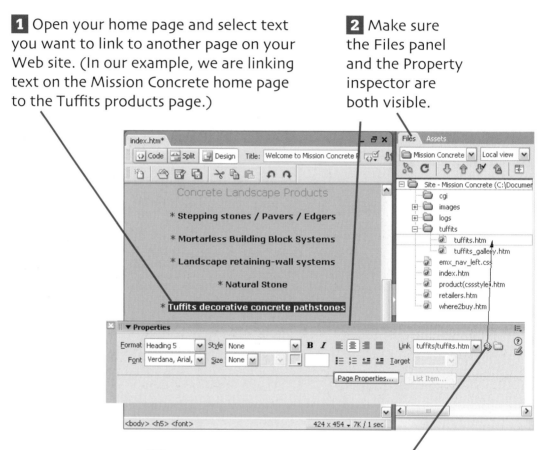

3 Click the compass-like Point to File icon and drag the line that appears to your to-be-linked file in the Files panel. Release your cursor and the file path for the other file will appear in the Link text window.

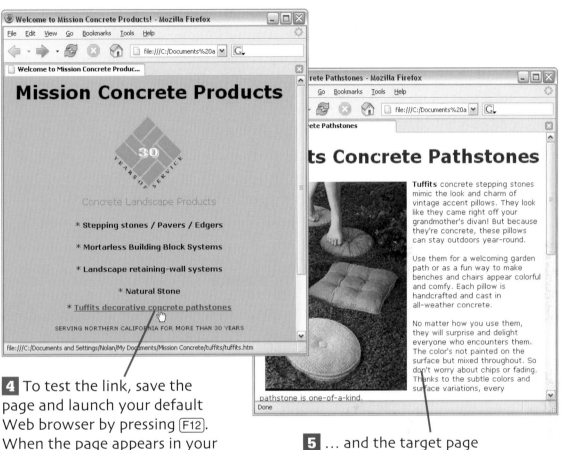

4 To test the link, save the page and launch your default Web browser by pressing F12. When the page appears in your browser, click the linked text...

5 ... and the target page will appear in your browser.

link text externally

Links to items not part of your own Web site are called external links. While we use text in this example, you can create external links using images as well. (See extra bits on page 71.)

1 Make sure the Files panel and Property inspector are visible, then select the text you want to link to a page out on the Web.

Tuffits concrete stepping stones mimic the look and charm of vintage accent pillows. They look like they came right off your grandmother's divan! But because they're concrete, these pillows can stay outdoors year-round.

Use them for a welcoming garden path or as a fun way to make benches and chairs appear colorful and comfy. As featured in the April 2004 issue of Sunset magazine, the pillows are handcrafted and cast in all-weather concrete.

▼ **Properties**

Format	Paragraph	Style	None	**B** *I*	≣ ≣ ≣ ≣	Link	http://www.sunset.com/sunset/in
Font	Verdana, Arial,	Size	2	pixels	#CC3300	≔ ≔ ≛ ≛	Target

Page Properties...

_blank
_parent
_self
_top

2 Type the full Web address for the outside page, including the http://, directly into the Link text window…

3 …then select _blank from the Target drop-down menu. Save the page and test the link in your browser, where the outside link will open in a new window.

color page links

By default, unvisited Web links are blue and underlined while visited links are purple and underlined. Dreamweaver, however, makes it easy to change the color and style of all your links to match your Web site's overall look. (See extra bits on page 71.)

1 Open your home page, which already contains a link, and click the Page Properties button in the Property inspector.

2 Select the Links category in the Page Properties dialog box. By default, the Link font is the same as the page's font and the link is underlined.

3 While you can change the font and size of the link text, in our example, we have changed only the colors used to indicate different link states: the Link color of the page's linked text; Visited links for after the link's been clicked; Rollover links for when the visitor's cursor hovers over the link without clicking it; and Active links for the moment when the link is clicked. Once you set the link colors and styles, click OK to apply the change and close the dialog box. Save the page before continuing.

color site links (cont.)

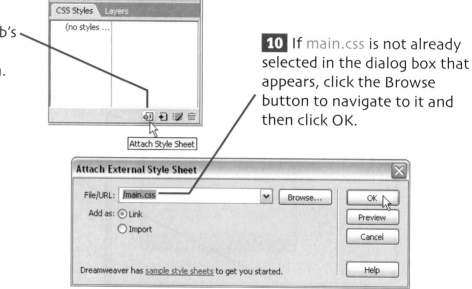

9 Click the CSS Styles tab's Attach Style Sheet button.

10 If main.css is not already selected in the dialog box that appears, click the Browse button to navigate to it and then click OK.

Attach Style Sheet

Attach External Style Sheet

File/URL: /main.css   Browse...   OK

Add as: ⦿ Link   Preview
⦾ Import   Cancel

Dreamweaver has sample style sheets to get you started.   Help

11 The main.css style sheet will immediately appear in the page's CSS Styles tab, indictating that it has been attached.

▼ Design
CSS Styles | Layers
⊟ main.css
  a:link   #CC3300
  a:visited   #990000
  a:hover   #FF3300
  a:active   #FF0033

12 You then can attach the main.css style sheet to any other page on your site.

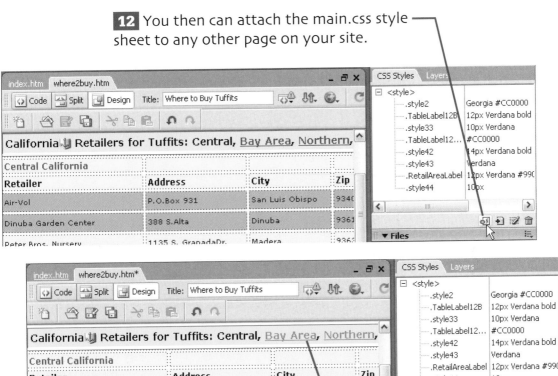

13 The main.css styles will be added to the page's existing styles and immediately change the color of the page's links.

add email link

By embedding addresses in your email links, you make it easy for readers to send email to you and others listed on your Web site. (See extra bits on page 71.)

1 Select the text on your page that you want to link to email. (In our example, we've selected Contact us! on the Mission Concrete home page.)

2 Click the Email button on the Insert toolbar.

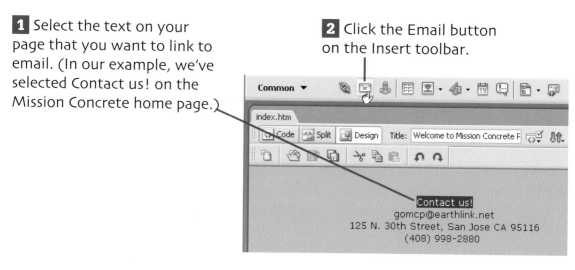

3 The selected text will be highlighted in the Email Link dialog box. Type the email address into the bottom text window and click OK.

4 The text selected on your page will become a link. Test it by saving the page, opening it in your Web browser and clicking the link. Your default email program will automatically create a new message addressed to the email address on the Web page.

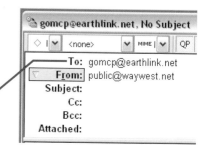

add anchor link

Anchor links enable Web visitors to jump to a specific spot within a long Web page, sparing readers from scrolling through it. You must first create an anchor to mark the particular spot in the target document. Then you create a link to that spot. (See extra bits on page 71.)

1 Open a Web page and click at the particular spot where you want to add an anchor link. (In our example, we're marking the start of our Northern California retailers in a list of suppliers.)

2 Click the Named Anchor button in the Insert toolbar.

3 Type a distinctive name in the Named Anchor dialog box and click OK.

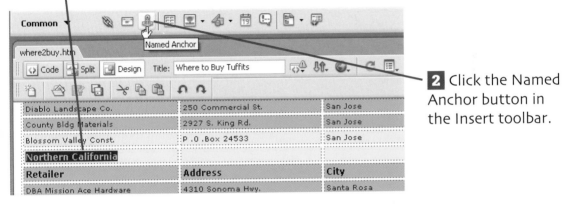

An anchor icon will be added next to the selected text. Save the page, which will also save the anchor name.

add anchor link (cont.)

4 Now select the text you want linked to the anchor.

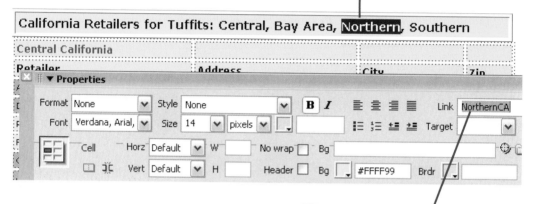

5 Type the anchor name exactly as you created it into the Property inspector's Link text window. (In our example, we're linking to the anchor we just created, NorthernCA.) Press Enter (Windows) or Return (Mac) to activate the link.

link image

Images are easy to spot on a page and easy to click, so don't limit yourself to creating just text links. Creating internal vs. external links with images works exactly as it does for text links. (See extra bits on page 71.)

With the Files panel and Property inspector both visible, open the page containing the image you want to link to something, and select it.

Use the Point to File icon to draw a line to the file you want to link the image to. (In our example, we are linking a button-sized image to our list of Tuffits retailers.)

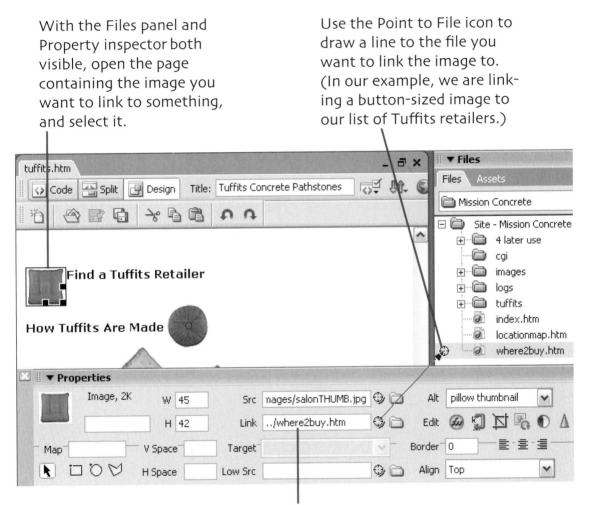

The file path for the other file will appear in the Link text window. Release your cursor to create the link.

create image map

Image maps take the basic idea behind an image link and give it extra power by making it possible to link separate "hot spots" within the image to multiple files. It saves space on the page and provides an elegant, easy-to-understand interface for your site. (See extra bits on page 72.)

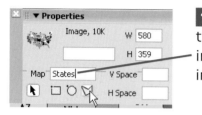

1 With the Property inspector visible, open the image for which you want to create an image map. Type a name for the image map in the Map text window.

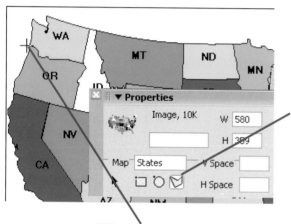

2 Based on the shape of the hot spot you'll be creating, click one of the three shape buttons. (In our example, we've chosen the freeform polygon to create an Oregon-shaped hot spot.)

3 Click in your image where you want to begin creating the hot spot, which will be marked by a cross-hair.

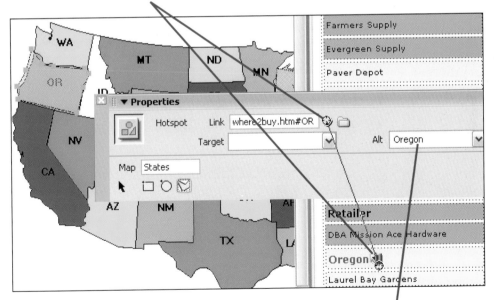

4 Build your hot spot one click at a time along the boundary of the underlying image.

5 If you need to adjust the hot spot's boundary, click any square-shaped handle and drag it to a new spot.

6 After building your hot spots, select one and use the Property inspector's Point to File icon to link it to a document. (In our example, we've linked to an anchor within the file.)

Farmers Supply

Evergreen Supply

Paver Depot

▼ Properties

Hotspot   Link where2buy.htm#OR

Target

Alt Oregon

Map States

Retailer

DBA Mission Ace Hardware

Oregon

Laurel Bay Gardens

7 Be sure to add an Alt name for the hot spot to help you keep them straight. Repeat these steps for each hot spot you've created, giving each its own Alt name.

create links

create image map (cont.)

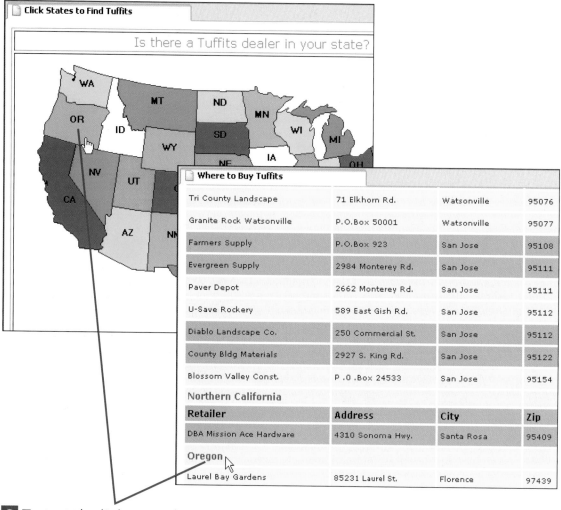

8 To test the link, save the page and launch your default Web browser by pressing F12. Click any of the image's hot spots and the linked page will appear in your browser.

extra bits

link text internally p. 56

- If the file to which you're linking is not already part of your Web site, click the Folder icon next to the Link drop-down menu and navigate to it. When Dreamweaver asks to import the file into the site, click Yes.

link text externally p. 58

- Reduce the chance of typing in the wrong Web address by copying the outside page's URL from your browser and pasting it directly into the Link text window.

- Selecting _blank from the Target drop-down menu will open a new window in the visitor's browser—ensuring that your site will remain visible as the visitor looks at the external Web page.

color page links p. 59

- Used since the birth of the Web, underlined blue and purple links are recognized by virtually all Web surfers. It's fine to change the color scheme but be prudent. Making unvisited links purple, for example, would be akin to making stop lights green.

- Our example uses shades of red for all four link states. The colors are different enough from each other to signal link-state changes

without creating a kaleidoscope of colors that might distract from the page's overall color scheme.

color site links p. 60

- In our example, we use the home page but you can replace the internal style sheet on any page on your site.

add email link p. 64

- With robot programs scouring the Web for email addresses, it's a sad fact that putting an email link on your Web site almost guarantees that your inbox will be flooded with spam. One workaround: enter your email as "myname AT earthlink DOT net" instead of as "myname@earthlink.net." For now, address-harvesting robots can't cope with this trick, while your human visitors will realize they need to replace the AT with @ and the DOT with a period.

extra bits

add anchor link p. 65

- The anchor can be placed anywhere and doesn't need to be tied to a text selection.

- Dreamweaver inserts the anchor-shaped icon next to your anchor-link text just to help you spot it. It will not be visible on your Web site. To turn these icons off or on, choose View > Visual Aids > Invisible Elements.

create image map p. 68

- Image map names should not include any blank spaces or special characters.

- The hot spot need not exactly match the underlying shape. Just cover the portion your visitors will most likely click.

- If you can't arrange your document windows to point directly to an anchor, use Browse to reach the file. Then type #nameofanchor at the end of the file name selected in the Link text window.

- As with text and images, a hot spot can link to an internal or external file.

6. reuse items to save time

Think of the Assets tab as Dreamweaver's grand central timesaver. It automatically lists which images, color swatches, and external links you use on your site. If you want to use those items again, the Assets tab makes it easy to quickly find what you need. The Assets tab also includes two other major timesavers— library items and templates, both of which we'll use in our project.

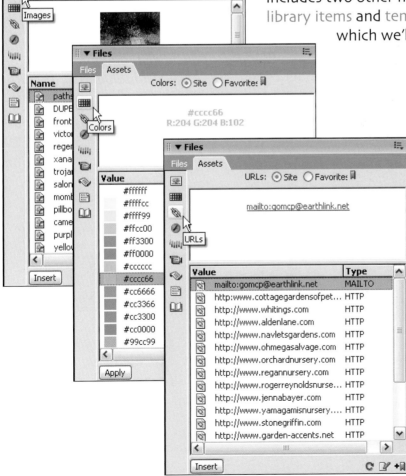

create a favorite

By creating favorites from the lists generated by the Assets tab, you always have your most-used items handy.

1 Press F11 to open the Assets tab and make sure the Site radio button is selected.

2 Select the category button you need in the left-hand column. (In our example, we've chosen the Images button because with so many images used, creating a shorter favorites list is essential.)

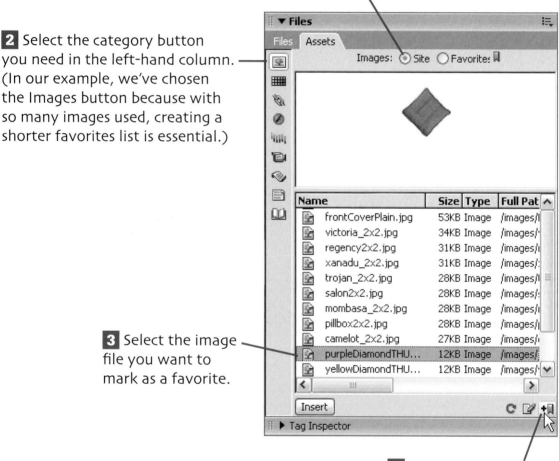

3 Select the image file you want to mark as a favorite.

4 Click the plus-marked Add Favorite icon at the bottom.

reuse items to save time

5 Click the Favorites radio button in the Assets tab.

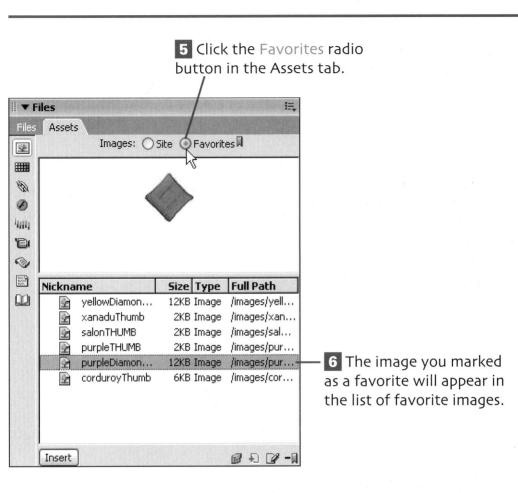

6 The image you marked as a favorite will appear in the list of favorite images.

create a library item

Make library items of anything you use repeatedly. It can be something simple like a 2 x 400-pixel rule. Or it can be as elaborate as an entire table containing images and links. Short or long, the real benefit of a library item comes when you need to make a change—change it once and all pages using it automatically update. (See extra bits on page 91.)

1 Select the Library category button in the Assets tab of the Files panel.

3 Click the Add icon at the bottom of the Assets tab.

2 Select the item you want to make into a library item. (In our example, it's a horizontal rule and copyright notice that we want to appear on every page.)

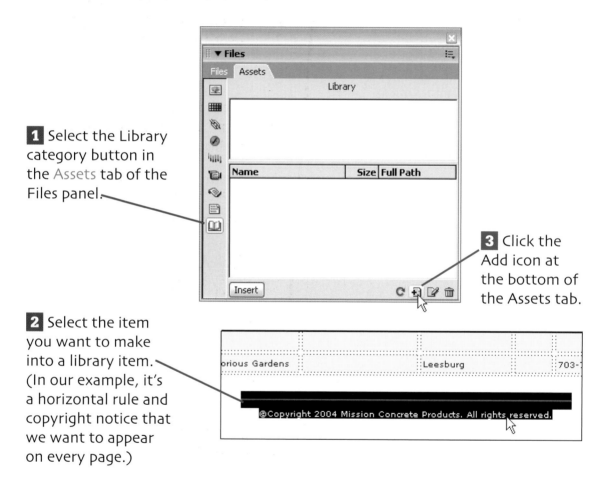

reuse items to save time

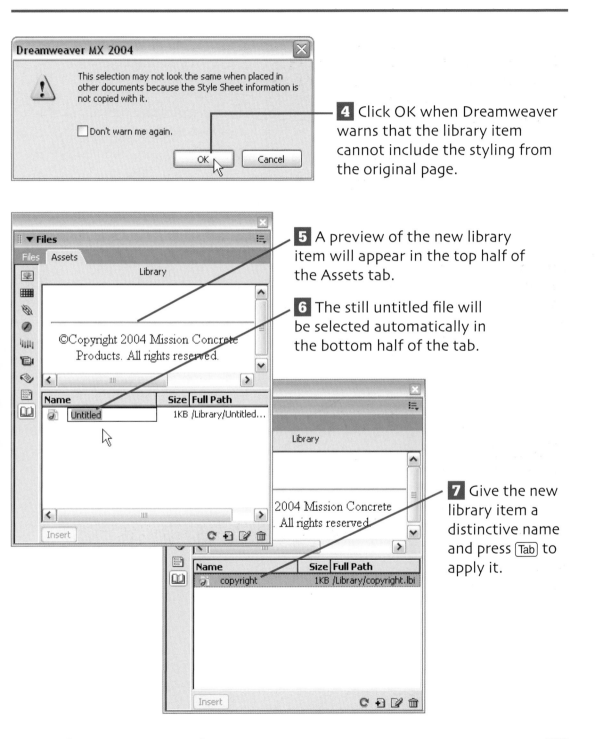

4 Click OK when Dreamweaver warns that the library item cannot include the styling from the original page.

5 A preview of the new library item will appear in the top half of the Assets tab.

6 The still untitled file will be selected automatically in the bottom half of the tab.

7 Give the new library item a distinctive name and press Tab to apply it.

edit library item

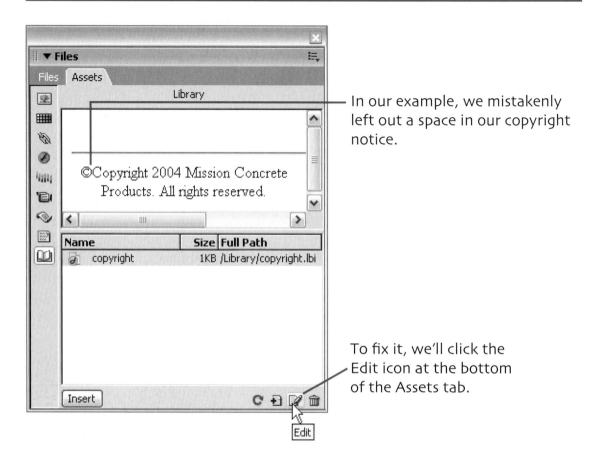

In our example, we mistakenly left out a space in our copyright notice.

To fix it, we'll click the Edit icon at the bottom of the Assets tab.

reuse items to save time

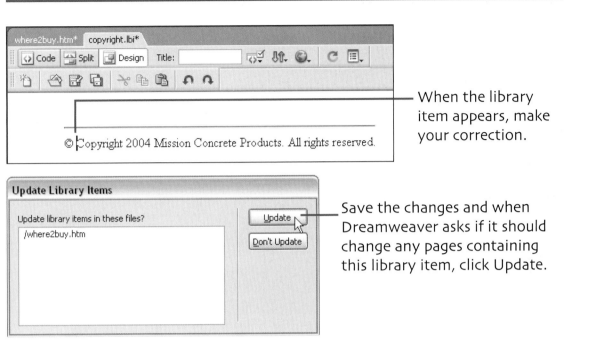

When the library item appears, make your correction.

Update Library Items

Update library items in these files?

/where2buy.htm

[Update]

[Don't Update]

Save the changes and when Dreamweaver asks if it should change any pages containing this library item, click Update.

When a dialog box appears listing which pages were updated, click Close. The Asset tab's preview of the library item will update to reflect the changes. Close the edited library page to get it out of your way.

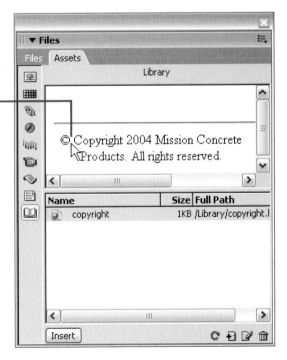

insert library item

Concrete Landscape Products

* **Stepping stones / Pavers / Edgers**

* **Mortarless Building Block Systems**

* **Landscape retaining-wall systems**

* **Natural Stone**

* **Tuffits decorative concrete pathstones**

SERVING NORTHERN CALIFORNIA FOR MORE THAN 30 YEARS

Contact us!
gomcp@earthlink.net
125 N. 30th Street, San Jose CA 95116
(408) 998-2880

Files

Files | Assets

Library

© 2004, Mission Concrete Products. All Rights Reserved.

Name	Size	Full Path
copyright	1KB	/Library/copyright.lbi

Insert

With the Assets tab of the Files panel open and visible, click in the open page where you want to place the selected library item...

...and then click the Asset tab's Insert button.

reuse items to save time

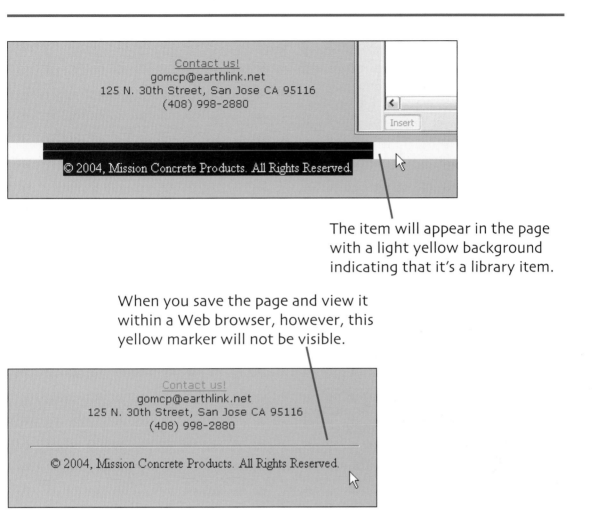

The item will appear in the page with a light yellow background indicating that it's a library item.

When you save the page and view it within a Web browser, however, this yellow marker will not be visible.

create a template

Templates are great timesavers for building pages with an identical layout but with variable content. In our example, we've created a Tuffits product template, which can then be used to generate pages for each product. Templates require that you mark which parts can be changed in the individual pages created from it. (See extra bits on page 91.)

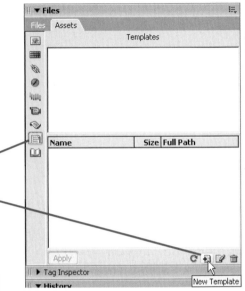

1 Select the Templates category button in the Assets tab and click the New Template button.

2 The still untitled file will be selected automatically in the bottom half of the tab. Give the new template item a distinctive name and press [Tab] to apply it. (In our example, we've named it product since we'll be using it as the template for all Tuffits products.)

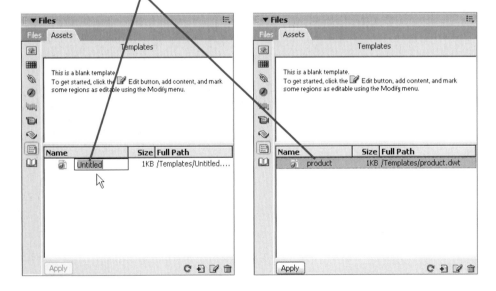

reuse items to save time

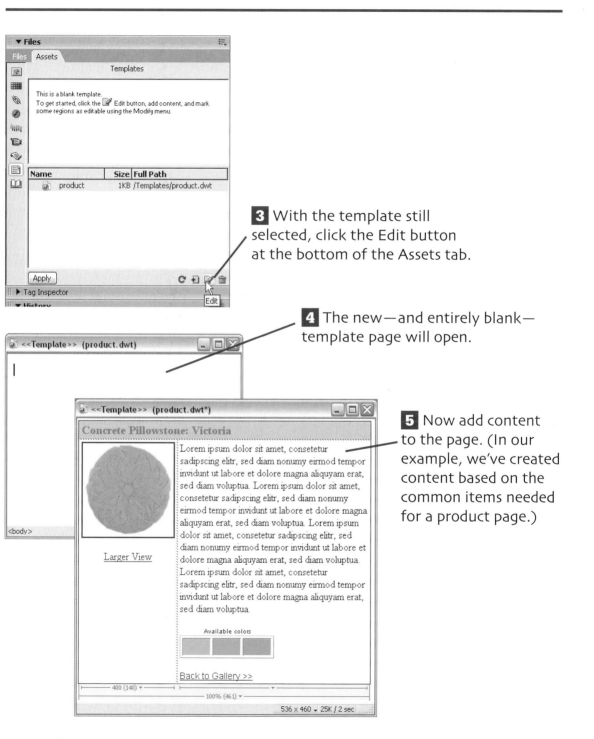

3 With the template still selected, click the Edit button at the bottom of the Assets tab.

4 The new—and entirely blank— template page will open.

5 Now add content to the page. (In our example, we've created content based on the common items needed for a product page.)

reuse items to save time

create a template (cont.)

6 Once you finish adding your content, you need to mark which items in the template can be changed, or edited. Make sure the Insert toolbar is set to Common, then select a page item (in our example, the main text block).

7 Click the Templates button in the toolbar and choose Editable Region in the drop-down menu.

8 When the New Editable Region dialog box appears, select the generic name in the Name text window, type in a more descriptive name, and click OK.

reuse items to save time

9 Your region name will be added to the template page.

10 Continue adding and naming editable regions until you're done.

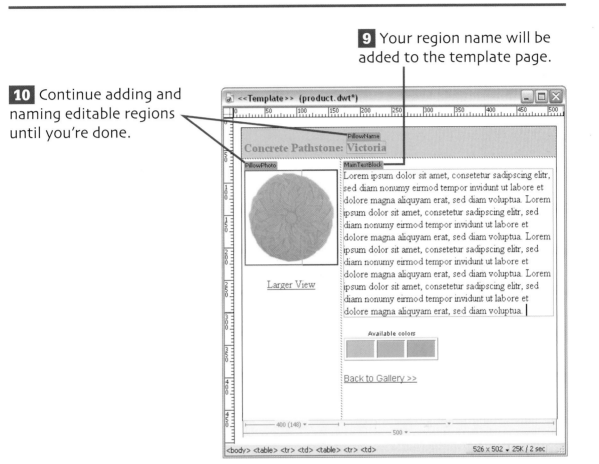

11 Save the template page and its content will appear in the upper half of the Assets tab. You can now start generating pages based on the template.

use your template

Once you create a template, you can generate as many individual pages as you
need based on its design.

Choose File > New and when the
New from Template dialog box
appears, select the Templates tab.

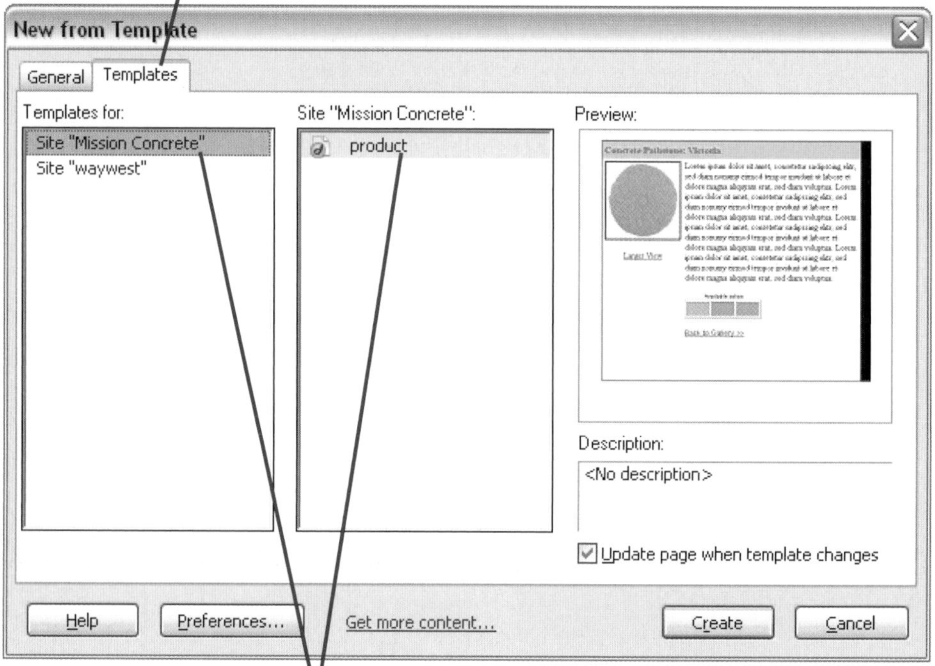

New from Template

General | Templates

Templates for:

Site "Mission Concrete"
Site "waywest"

Site "Mission Concrete":

📄 product

Preview:

Description:

<No description>

☑ Update page when template changes

| Help | Preferences... | Get more content... | | Create | Cancel |

Choose your site in the first column,
select the template you just created in
the second column, and click Create.

reuse items to save time

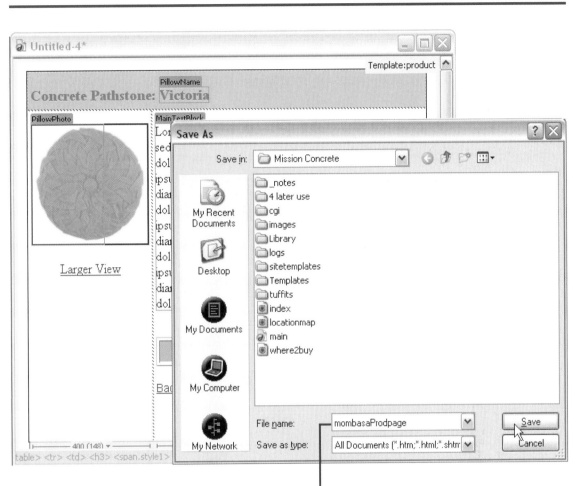

When a new untitled page based on the template appears, save it and give it a new name. (In our example, we've named the page mombasaProdpage to reflect its eventual content.) Be sure to also give the new page a title, which will be blank initially since it's a template-based page.

use your template (cont.)

You now can begin to replace the page's editable regions, marked with teal-colored names, with content tailored to the individual page.

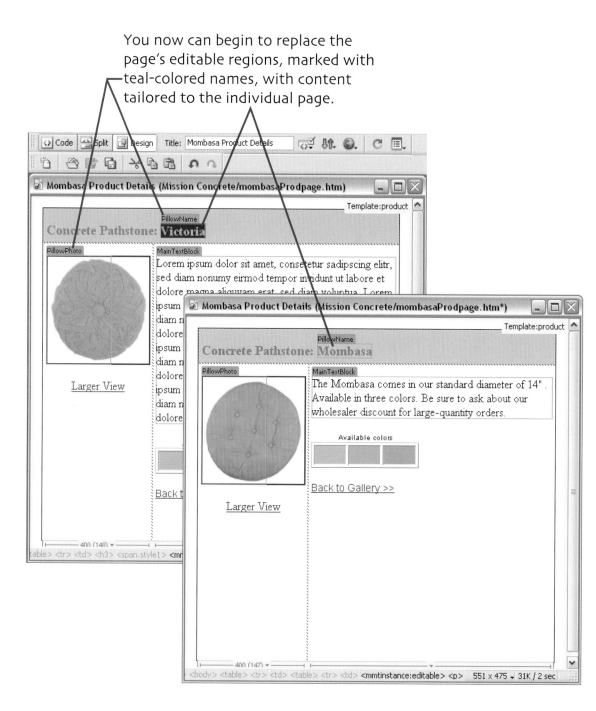

edit template

Here's the real payoff for building individual pages based on a template: You can change the template and all the pages will be updated automatically.

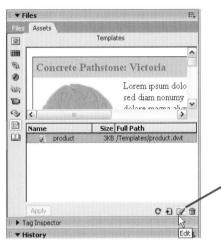

Open the template that you need to change by selecting it in the Assets tab and clicking the Edit button.

Once the template opens, make the needed changes. (In our example, we've changed the header to a color more in keeping with the Tuffits pillow palette, using the Property inspector.)

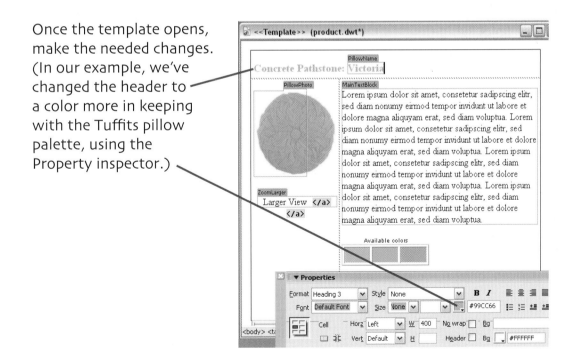

edit template (cont.)

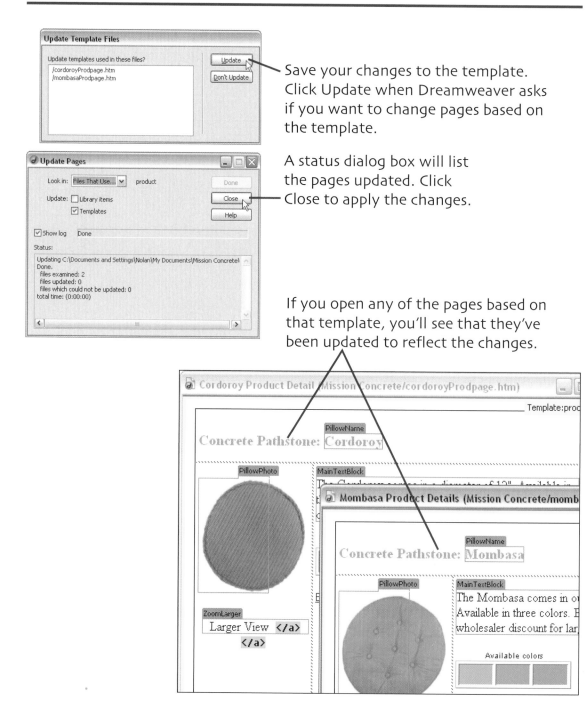

Save your changes to the template. Click Update when Dreamweaver asks if you want to change pages based on the template.

A status dialog box will list the pages updated. Click Close to apply the changes.

If you open any of the pages based on that template, you'll see that they've been updated to reflect the changes.

reuse items to save time

extra bits

create a library item p. 76

- The horizontal rule and copyright notice can be a single library item because they sit next to each other. If they were in two different spots on the page, they'd have to be made into two separate library items.

- While library items contain no styling themselves, they can contain references to style sheets. Use external style sheets to keep library items consistently styled, as explained on page 60.

- Dreamweaver will automatically add the .lbi suffix to a library item file name, designating the file as a library item.

create a template p. 82

- By default, every item on a template is initially locked, that is, not editable. Only the items you specifically mark as editable will be available for changes.

- When you save the template, Dreamweaver automatically adds a .dwt suffix. Dreamweaver sometimes will ask if you want to update any pages using it—even though you haven't built any such pages yet. Just click Yes to close the dialog box.

reuse items to save time

7. add navigation

As your Web site grows in size, visitors need an easy way to move from page to page, or even section to section. By including a navigation bar, often called a Nav-bar, on all your pages, visitors can move around your site without getting lost.

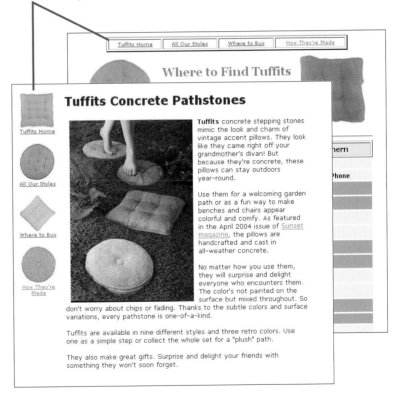

We will start by adding a Nav-bar to your site's home page. (In our example, we're adding it to the tuffits page.) Before we add the Nav-bar, however, we're going to create two layers—one to hold the Nav-bar and one for the main area of the Web page.

add layers

Originally, Web designers were forced to use cumbersome tables or framesets to lay out magazine-style Web pages. But now that most Web browsers support style sheet positioning tags, you can use layers. In Dreamweaver, using layers is a click-and-drag affair.

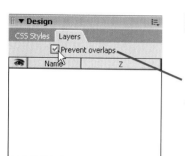

1 Switch the Insert toolbar to Layout using the drop-down menu. Press F2 to open the Layers tab of the Design panel and check Prevent overlaps.

2 Open your site's home page (in our example, the top-level tuffits page). Select the entire page and then cut it (Ctrl X in Windows, Cmd X on the Mac).

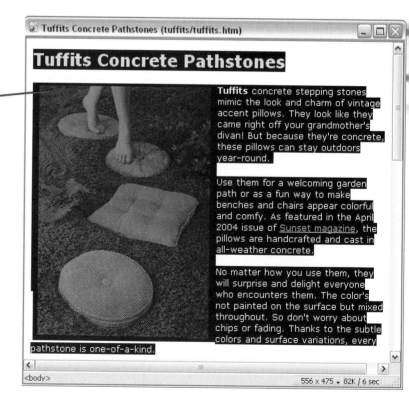

Tuffits Concrete Pathstones (tuffits/tuffits.htm)

Tuffits Concrete Pathstones

Tuffits concrete stepping stones mimic the look and charm of vintage accent pillows. They look like they came right off your grandmother's divan! But because they're concrete, these pillows can stay outdoors year-round.

Use them for a welcoming garden path or as a fun way to make benches and chairs appear colorful and comfy. As featured in the April 2004 issue of Sunset magazine, the pillows are handcrafted and cast in all-weather concrete.

No matter how you use them, they will surprise and delight everyone who encounters them. The color's not painted on the surface but mixed throughout. So don't worry about chips or fading. Thanks to the subtle colors and surface variations, every pathstone is one-of-a-kind.

<body>   556 x 475 ▾ 82K / 6 sec

add navigation

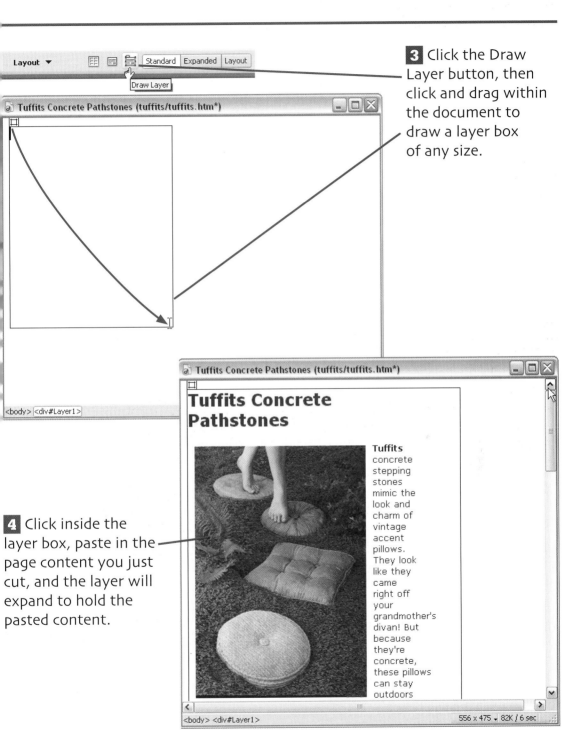

3 Click the Draw Layer button, then click and drag within the document to draw a layer box of any size.

Draw Layer

Layout ▼ Standard | Expanded | Layout

Tuffits Concrete Pathstones (tuffits/tuffits.htm*)

`<body> <div#Layer1>`

4 Click inside the layer box, paste in the page content you just cut, and the layer will expand to hold the pasted content.

Tuffits Concrete Pathstones (tuffits/tuffits.htm*)

Tuffits Concrete Pathstones

Tuffits concrete stepping stones mimic the look and charm of vintage accent pillows. They look like they came right off your grandmother's divan! But because they're concrete, these pillows can stay outdoors

`<body> <div#Layer1>`

556 x 475 ▾ 82K / 6 sec

add navigation

add layers (cont.)

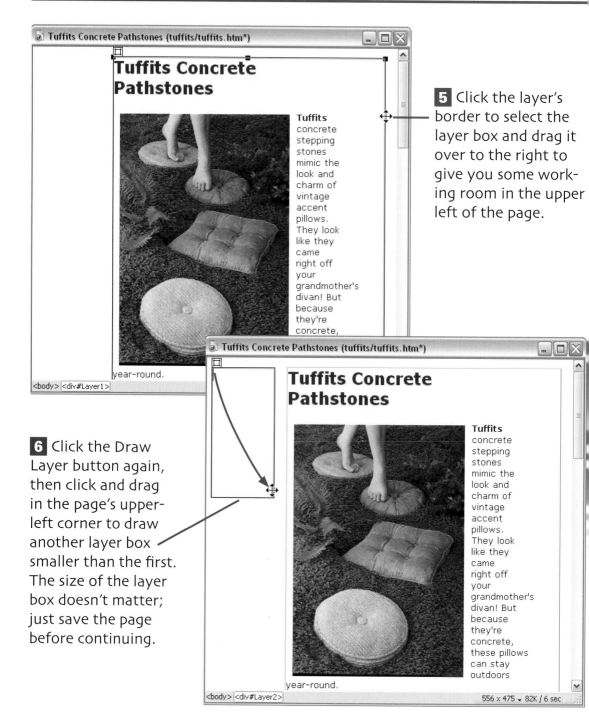

5 Click the layer's border to select the layer box and drag it over to the right to give you some working room in the upper left of the page.

6 Click the Draw Layer button again, then click and drag in the page's upper-left corner to draw another layer box smaller than the first. The size of the layer box doesn't matter; just save the page before continuing.

name layers

We're going to give these layers real names to better distinguish them from one another. (See extra bits on page 110.)

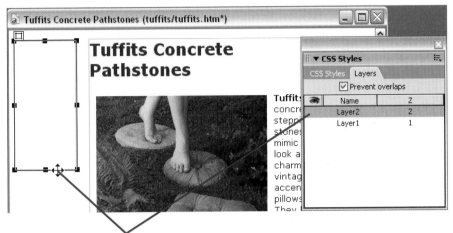

Click the left layer's border to select it and it will be highlighted in the Layers tab.

Double-click the layer's listing in the Layers tab. (In our example, it's Layer2.)

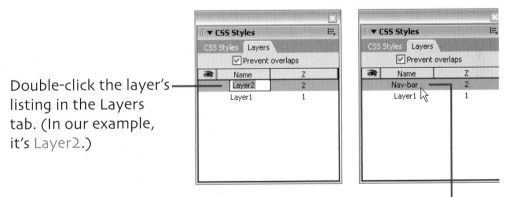

Type in a more descriptive name and press [Tab] to apply it. (In our example, we've named it Nav-bar since that's what this will become.) Select the other layer and give it a more descriptive name as well. (We'll use MainBlock.)

position layers

Now we're ready to put the layers exactly where we need them for what will become the Nav-bar. (See extra bits on page 110.)

1 Make sure the Property inspector and rulers are visible. Select the Nav-bar layer and take a look at two of the Property inspector's text windows: L and T, which denote how far in px (pixels) the layer sits from the Left Top corner of the page. (In our example, the layer is 8 pixels to the right and 15 pixels below the top-left corner.)

2 The absolute corner would be L: 0 and T: 0, which is where we want our Nav-bar layer to start. Type in those numbers and press (Tab). The Nav-bar layer will tuck itself into the top-left corner.

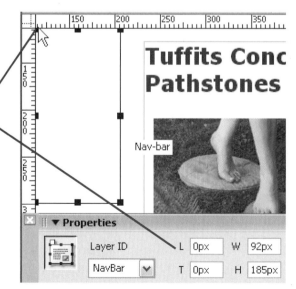

3 The W and H text windows in the Property inspector set the layer's Width and Height. (In our example, we want the Nav-bar to be exactly 100 pixels wide, not 92 as it is on the left, and since we're not sure how high it needs to be, we'll type in 600 to be safe.)

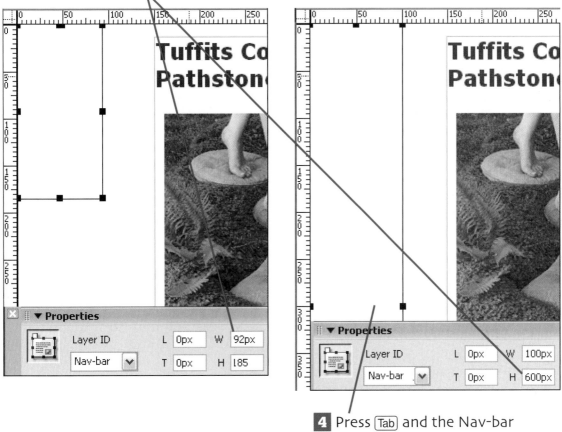

4 Press Tab and the Nav-bar layer will be resized.

position layers (cont.)

5 With the Nav-bar layer positioned, we now can put the MainBlock layer exactly where it belongs. The Nav-bar layer's L value is 0 and it's 100 pixels wide, so we'll set the MainBlock's L value at 105, which gives us a 5-pixel gutter for a bit of breathing room. Press Tab to apply the change and jump to the T text window.

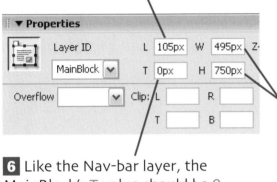

6 Like the Nav-bar layer, the MainBlock's T value should be 0 so that the layers line up across the top of the page. Press Tab to apply the change and jump to the W text window.

7 Finally, we'll set the MainBlock layer width at 495 (100+5+495=600, to easily fit on most monitors). Press Tab to jump to the H text window, where we'll set the height at a generous 750 pixels since Web browsers let viewers scroll down deep windows. Press Tab and you're done. Save your work before continuing.

create main nav-bar

With the Nav-bar layer placed where we need it, adding the content is the easy part. (See extra bits on page 110.)

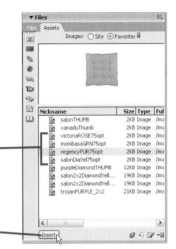

1 If you haven't already, create a series of images small enough to fit inside your new Nav-bar. (In our example, we've taken images of Tuffits pillows, reduced them to 75 pixels wide, and resampled them.)

2 Click in the Nav-bar, and click the Asset tab's Insert button. The selected image will appear in the Nav-bar.

3 Right after the first Nav-bar image, add a line break, type in a short label for what will become your first text link, and then start a new paragraph. Don't bother with styling any of this just yet. Instead, repeat these steps to add the other images and link labels you need for each of your site's main areas of interest.

4 Select the first text label and style it as needed. (In our example, Dreamweaver named it style3, with the text set at 10 pixels so that it will fit better in the narrow Nav-bar.)

5 Rename the Nav-bar text style. (In our example, we've renamed it NavbarLabel for clarity.) Apply the style to the rest of the Nav-bar text labels.

create main nav-bar (cont.)

6 Use the Property inspector to center all the Nav-bar content.

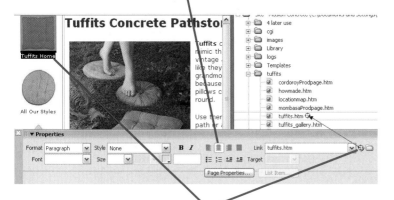

7 Since the Nav-bar's first image and text label will link to the same page, select them both and make the link using the Property inspector. (In our example, we're linking to tuffits.)

8 While the text reflects the link colors we set in our external style sheet (main.css), the linked image shows a big border in the Web browser view that interferes with the Nav-bar's otherwise clean look.

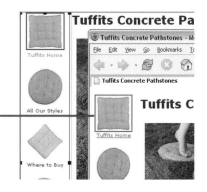

9 Fortunately, the fix is easy: eliminate the border. Select the image and you'll see that the Property inspector's Border setting is blank—the default setting—but not, surprisingly, the same as zero. Type a 0 (zero) into the Border's text window and press [Tab] to apply the change.

10 Save the page and view it in your Web browser. Now the border really is gone!

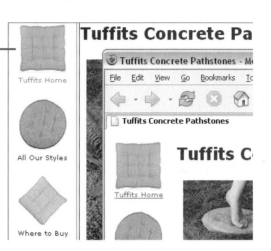

11 Link the rest of your Nav-bar images and text, set each image border to zero, and your Nav-bar stands ready on your home page to guide visitors through the site.

create small nav-bar

You could place the Nav-bar you just created on every page of the site. But in case you don't want to use that much space on every page for a Nav-bar, we'll create a small, table-based Nav-bar styled much like its home-page cousin. This task pulls together many of the skills you've learned and shows how you can use Dreamweaver to quickly build relatively complex pages.

1 Open your home page, look in the CSS Styles tab, and select the label style you created for the main Nav-bar. (In our example, we've selected NavbarLabel.)

2 Right-click (Windows) or Ctrl-click (Mac) the label style and choose Export from the drop-down menu. When the Export Styles As CSS File dialog box appears, name the exported style nav-barStyle, and click Save.

CSS Styles

CSS Styles	Layers

- main.css
  - a:link — Verdana #CC0000 border: 0px none
  - a:visited — #990000
  - a:hover — #FF3300
  - a:active — #CC3366
  - .footer — 12px Verdana font-style: normal line
- <style>
  - body — background-color: #FFFFFF

Files

3 Open a page where you want to use a smaller Nav-bar and click the CSS Styles tab's Attach Style Sheet button.

4 Click Browse when the Attach External Style Sheet dialog box appears.

Attach External Style Sheet

File/URL: ../main.css

Browse... OK

Add as: ● Link   Preview
○ Import   Cancel

Dreamweaver has sample style sheets to get you started.   Help

Select Style Sheet File

Select file name from: ● File system   Sites and Servers...
○ Data sources

Look in: Mission Concrete

- _notes   Templates
- 4 later use tuffits
- cgi   main
- images   nav-barStyle
- Library
- logs

File name: nav-barStyle   OK

Files of type: Style Sheet Files (*.css)   Cancel

URL: ../nav-barStyle.css

Relative to: Document

5 When the Select Style Sheet File dialog box appears, select nav-barStyle and click OK to close the dialog box.

create small nav-bar (cont.)

6 When the Attach External Style Sheet dialog box reappears, click OK again to close it as well. The nav-barStyle style sheet now appears in your page's CSS Styles tab.

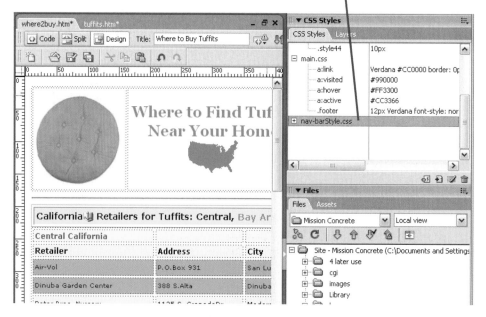

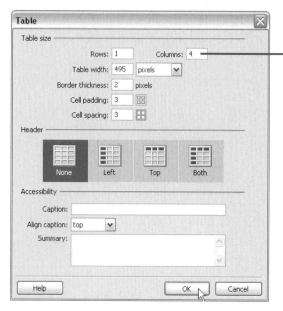

7 Now insert a table at the very top of the page. (In our example, we inserted a 495-pixel wide table with one row and four columns, which will match the number of links in the main nav-bar.)

add navigation

8 Select and center the table when it appears on the page. In the table's first cell, add the text for your first link. Don't worry when the cell widths shift around as you do this.

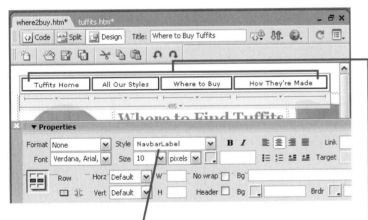

9 Add link text to the rest of the cells, select them all, and in the Property inspector choose the NavbarLabel in the Style drop-down menu.

10 All the selected text will change to that style.

create small nav-bar (cont.)

11 Use the Property inspector to link the text in each cell to your site's main pages. ⎯⎯

12 As you do so, the links will be styled based on the nav-barStyle style sheet you attached to the page. ⎯⎯

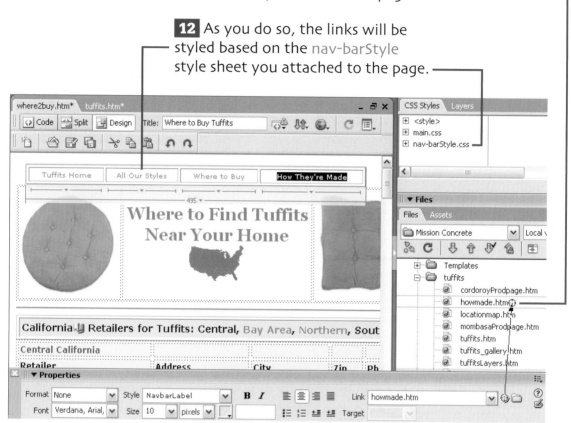

13 After you've linked all the labels in the table, save your work.

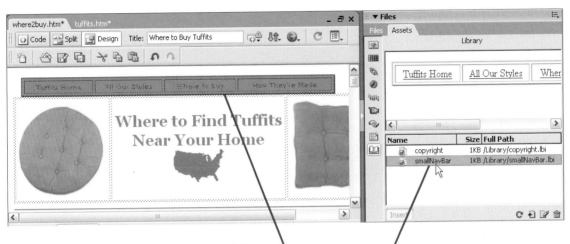

14 Select the table, turn it into a library item with a clear name, and you'll be able to add this space-saving Nav-bar to any page that includes the nav-barStyle style sheet.

extra bits

name layers p. 97

- You also can select a layer by clicking its name in the Layers tab.

position layers p. 98

- You also can select a layer and drag it where you want it, but for precise positioning use the Property inspector's text windows.

create main nav-bar p. 101

- While the first link is to the home page itself, that's not really a problem. If visitors viewing the home page click the link, they remain right where they are.

8. publish site

Finally, you're ready to put your pages on the Web, a process sometimes called publishing since they'll become available for anyone to read. Dreamweaver's expanded Files panel plays a key role in helping you keep track of which files are where and when they were last changed.

Macromedia Dreamweaver MX 2004 - [Tuffits Concrete Pathstones (tuffits/tuffits.htm)]

File   Edit   View   Site

Show: Mission Concrete

Remote Site	Size	Type	Modified
/webdocs/			
index.htm	4KB	HTM File	9/17/2004 1:27 AM
nav-barStyle.css	1KB	Cascadi...	9/16/2004 6:19 PM
main.css	1KB	Cascadi...	9/16/2004 6:17 PM
tuffits		Folder	9/16/2004 8:44 PM
where2buy.htm	25KB	HTM File	9/16/2004 6:41 PM
tuffits_galler...	5KB	HTM File	9/16/2004 7:03 PM
tuffits.htm	5KB	HTM File	9/16/2004 8:45 PM
retailers2.htm	10KB	HTM File	9/16/2004 8:54 PM
mombasaPro...	3KB	HTM File	9/16/2004 6:41 PM
locationmap....	2KB	HTM File	9/16/2004 6:20 PM
howmade.htm	3KB	HTM File	9/16/2004 6:41 PM
cordoroyProd...	3KB	HTM File	9/16/2004 6:41 PM
logs		Folder	9/16/2004 6:22 PM
Library		Folder	9/16/2004 6:20 PM
images		Folder	9/16/2004 6:42 PM
cgi		Folder	1/14/2004 12:00 AM

Local Files	Size	Type	Modified
Site - Mission Concrete (C:\Docu...		Folder	9/16/2004 6:57 PM
index.htm	4KB	HTM File	9/16/2004 6:57 PM
nav-barStyle.css	1KB	Cascad...	9/16/2004 6:19 PM
main.css	1KB	Cascad...	9/16/2004 6:17 PM
tuffits		Folder	9/16/2004 1:53 PM
where2buy.htm	25KB	HTM File	9/16/2004 1:43 PM
tuffits_gallery.htm	5KB	HTM File	9/16/2004 1:43 PM
tuffits.htm	5KB	HTM File	9/16/2004 8:45 PM
retailers2.htm	10KB	HTM File	9/16/2004 8:54 PM
mombasaProdpage.htm	3KB	HTM File	9/16/2004 1:43 PM
locationmap.htm	2KB	HTM File	9/16/2004 6:20 PM
howmade.htm	3KB	HTM File	9/16/2004 1:43 PM
cordoroyProdpage.htm	3KB	HTM File	9/16/2004 1:43 PM
Templates		Folder	9/16/2004 1:43 PM
logs		Folder	2/19/2004 5:46 PM
LOCAL ONLY		Folder	9/16/2004 11:12 ...
Library		Folder	9/16/2004 1:43 PM
images		Folder	9/15/2004 7:08 PM
cgi		Folder	2/19/2004 5:44 PM

1 local items selected totalling 4461 bytes.

add search terms

Help Web search engines highlight your site by entering a succinct description, along with multiple keywords, in the home page. Dreamweaver places this information in the page's hidden head code. (See extra bits on page 123.)

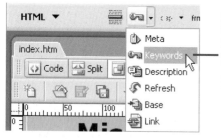

1 Open your home page and switch the Insert toolbar to HTML using the drop-down menu. Click the second button from the left and choose Keywords from its drop-down menu.

2 When the Keywords dialog box appears, type words that you think people might use to search for your site. Once you're done, click OK to close the dialog box.

3 Click the the second button from the left again and choose Description from its drop-down menu.

4 When the Description dialog box appears, type in a short paragraph that sums up the purpose of your Web site and the products it displays. Once you're done, click OK to close the dialog box.

5 If you want to see the otherwise hidden keywords and description, click the Split button. The terms appear as part of the meta data in the page's head code.

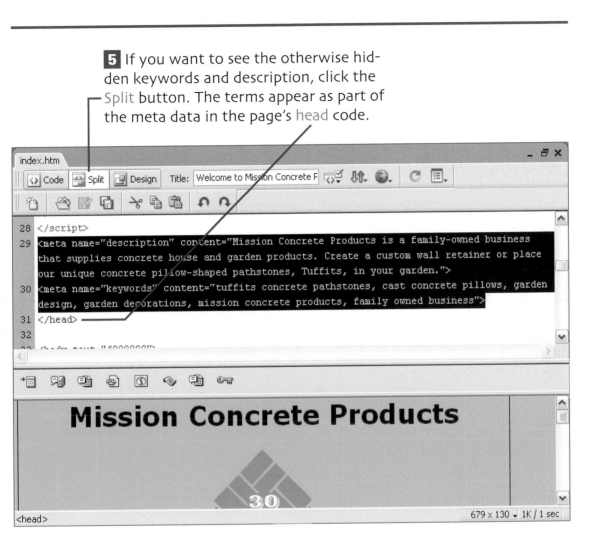

check and fix links

Few things are more frustrating for Web users than broken links. Dreamweaver can check your entire site in seconds and save everyone hours of frustration.

1 Choose Site > Check Links Sitewide and the Results panel will list any pages with broken links. (In our example, Dreamweaver found a link we deliberately mistyped, tuffBREAK.)

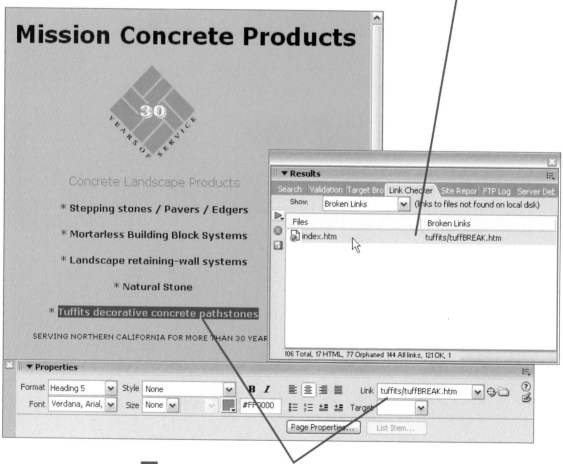

2 Double-click the file listing and Dreamweaver will open the Property inspector, along with the page that contains the broken link.

3 Use the Property inspector's Link window to correct the mistake by typing in the correct link or redrawing the link with the Point-to-File button.

Mission Concrete Products

▼ Results

Search | Validation | Target Bro | Link Checker | Site Repor | FTP Log | Server Det

Show: Broken Links | (links to files not found on local disk)

Files	Broken Links

106 Total, 17 HTML, 77 Orphaned 14 All links, 122 OK, 0

* Natural Stone

* Tuffits decorative concrete pathstones

Site - Mission Concrete (C:\Documents
- 4 later use
- cgi
- images
- Library
- logs
- Templates
- tuffits
  - advertiser.htm
  - cordoroyProdpage.htm
  - howmade.htm
  - locationmap.htm
  - mombasaProdpage.htm
  - tuffits.htm
  - tuffits_gallery.htm
  - tuffitsLayers.htm
  - where2buy.htm
- main.css
- nav-barStyle.css
- index.htm

▼ Properties

Format Heading 5 | Style None | **B** *I* | Link tuffits/tuffits.htm
Font Verdana, Arial, | Size None | #FF0000 | Target

Page Properties... | List Item...

4 Once you make the fix, save the page and the Results panel automatically removes the previously broken link from its list. Repeat until you've fixed all broken links.

explore the files panel

The Files panel serves as your main tool to put files from your local site on to the remote Web site. You also use it to get any of your remote files if, for example, you've accidentally deleted their local site counterparts. (See extra bits on page 123.)

Normally the Files panel only shows your local files. Click the Expand/Collapse button to see them along with your remote Web site's files.

The toolbar running above the file listings contains all the buttons needed to move files between the two locations.

The expanded view of the Files panel shows your remote and local files.

Click the
Connect/Disconnect
button to open or close
a live connection to the
remote Web site.

Click the Put files
button to move
selected files from
your local site to
the remote site.

Click the Get files
button to move
selected files from
the remote site to
the local site.

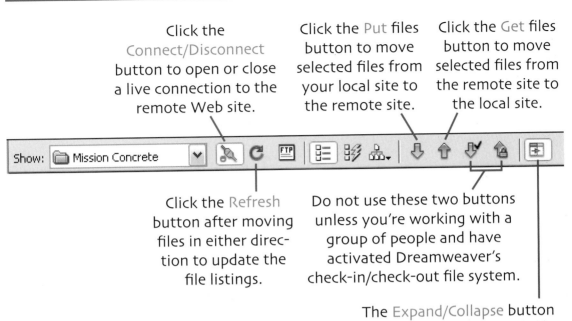

Click the Refresh
button after moving
files in either direc-
tion to update the
file listings.

Do not use these two buttons
unless you're working with a
group of people and have
activated Dreamweaver's
check-in/check-out file system.

The Expand/Collapse button
lets you see the remote and
local files, or just the local files.

publish site

connect to remote site

After double-checking your files, you're ready to place them on your remote site. Since you already entered the remote site's address details back in Chapter 1, you're ready to connect. (See extra bits on page 123.)

1 Unless you have an always-on connection to the Internet, activate your computer's dial-up connection now.

2 Return to Dreamweaver, make sure the Files panel is visible, and click the Expand/Collapse button.

3 Once the view expands, click the Connect button.

Macromedia Dreamweaver MX 2004								
File Edit View Site								
Show: [ ] Mission Concrete								

Remote Site	Size	Type	Modified	Local Files	Size	Type	Modified
To see your remote files, click the button on the toolbar.				Site - Mission Concrete (C:...		Folder	9/15/2004 7:03 P
				4 later use		Folder	9/13/2004 9:19 P
				cgi		Folder	2/19/2004 5:44 P
				examples		Folder	9/15/2004 7:08 P
				preOptimized		Folder	9/8/2004 8:27 PM
				tuffitsEarlier.htm	6KB	HTM File	9/15/2004 7:06 P
				images		Folder	9/15/2004 7:08 P
				Library		Folder	9/15/2004 7:15 P
				logs		Folder	2/19/2004 5:46 P
				Templates		Folder	9/5/2004 9:14 PM
				product.dwt	3KB	DWT File	9/5/2004 9:14 PM
				tuffits		Folder	9/15/2004 7:19 P
				main.css	1KB	Cascadin...	9/10/2004 2:31 P
				nav-barStyle.css	1KB	Cascadin...	9/10/2004 3:37 P
				index.htm	3KB	HTM File	9/14/2004 3:46 P

publish site

4 The Status dialog box will appear briefly as Dreamweaver negotiates the connection to your Web site.

Status

Retrieving remote folder information for tulfits.

[Cancel]

5 Once the connection is made, the remote site's files will appear in the left side of the Files panel. (In our example, we haven't put any files on the site yet, so all you see is the top-level folder, webdocs, and two don't–touch subfolders, cgi and logs.)

Remote Site	Size	Type
/webdocs/		
cgi		
logs		

Local Files	Size	Type	Modified
Site - Mission Concrete (C:...		Folder	9/15/2004 7:03 P
4 later use		Folder	9/13/2004 9:19 P
cgi		Folder	2/19/2004 5:44 P
examples		Folder	9/15/2004 7:08 P
images		Folder	9/15/2004 7:08 P
Library		Folder	9/15/2004 7:15 P
logs		Folder	2/19/2004 5:46 P
Templates		Folder	9/5/2004 9:14 PN
tuffits		Folder	9/15/2004 7:19 P
main.css	1KB	Cascadin...	9/10/2004 2:31 P
nav-barStyle.css	1KB	Cascadin...	9/10/2004 3:37 P
index.htm	3KB	HTM File	9/14/2004 3:46 P

6 You're ready to upload your files.

publish site

upload multiple files

If this is the first upload to your Web site, you'll be publishing multiple files, including all the necessary images for your pages. (See extra bits on page 123.)

1 Select the home page, index, in the Local Files pane and click the Put button to begin the upload.

You also can select individual files or folders by [Ctrl]-clicking (Windows) or [Cmd]-clicking (Mac) them in the Local Files pane. Click the Put button to upload them.

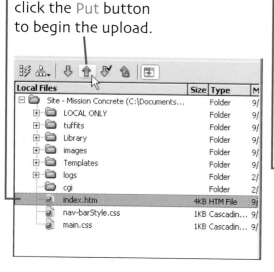

2 When Dreamweaver asks if you want to include dependent files, click Yes. Dependent files include every file and image linked, directly or indirectly, to the selected page(s). (In our example, this would include not only the index page, but also the attached main.css style sheet.)

3 A series of progress dialog boxes will flash by as Dreamweaver uploads the home page and all its dependent files. This may take several minutes to complete, depending on how many files you're uploading and the speed of your Internet connection.

120

4 When the progress dialog boxes stop appearing, press the Refresh button...

5 ...and then compare names of the Remote Site files to the names of your Local Files.

6 Check how the remote site pages look in your Web browser to make sure their appearance matches that of your local files. If you find mismatches, upload the local files again.

7 Once you're done, click the Disconnect button.

upload a single page

Sometimes you'll need to upload only a single page—for example, when you need to update information or fix a mistake. (See extra bits on page 123.)

1 Once you're connected, click the page file in the Local Files pane and drag it to the folder where the older version appears in the Remote Site pane.

2 When Dreamweaver asks if you want to include dependent files, click No. A single progress dialog box will appear as Dreamweaver uploads the selected page. Use your Web browser to check the page on the remote Web site, and when you're done, click the Disconnect button.

122

publish site

extra bits

add search terms p. 112

- When picking keywords and a description, especially for an uncommon product or service, think of similar products or services and use words people would most likely type in to find them.

explore the files panel p. 116

- If you are working solo, the check-in/check-out system is cumbersome since it forces you to alert yourself that you're using a file.

connect to remote site p. 118

- The local and remote versions of the cgi and logs folders are different since they reflect the specific activities for each set of files. If you try to replace one with the other, Dreamweaver will cancel the transfer.

upload multiple files p. 120

- While you could select your local site's top-level folder (in this case, Mission Concrete) and upload the whole thing, it's not recommended. You run the risk of publishing files you're still working on, not to mention wiping out remote files not found on your local site. Instead, it's best to upload only the local files and folders you specifically select.

upload a single page p. 122

- Since you've only changed the HTML file, there's no need to upload the dependent files that are already on the remote site.

index

A

Accessibility section, Table dialog box, 53
active links, 59
Add Favorite icon, 74
Add icon, 76
Adobe Photoshop Elements, xiii
Align Center icon, 12, 13
Align drop-down menu, 24, 32, 34, 35
Alt text box, 24, 26, 35, 69
anchor icon, 65, 71
anchor links, 65–66, 71
Assets tab, 73–85
    and favorites, 74–75
    and library items, 76–81
    purpose of, 3, 73
    and templates, 82–83, 85
Attach External Style Sheet dialog box, 105, 106
Attach Style Sheet button, 62, 105
author's Web site, xii

B

background color, 20, 81
background images, 20
Basic Page column, 10, 22
Bold icon, 15
Border box, Property inspector, 24, 102
borders
    image, 24, 102
    table, 39
breaks, line/paragraph, 15, 32, 101

Brightness and Contrast button, 29
Brightness slider, 29, 35
broken links, 114–115
browsers. See Web browsers
bulleted lists, 9, 18–19

C

Cascading Style Sheets, 22. See also CSS
Cell padding/spacing options, 46
cgi folder, 123
check-in/check-out file system, 8, 117, 123
Check Links Sitewide command, 114
Code view, 2
color
    for links, 59–63, 71
    for page background, 20
    for tables, 50, 53
    for text, 13
Color Picker, 13
comma-delimited data, 53
Common option, Insert toolbar, 25, 55, 84
companion Web site, xii
Connect/Disconnect button, 117, 118, 121, 122
connection, testing online, 7, 8
contact information, Web site, 15
Contrast slider, 29
copyright notice, 78–79, 91
Create New column, 22
creating
    alternate text for images, 24, 26, 35

headings for home pages, 16–17, 22
home pages, 10–11
image links, 67–70
library items, 76–77, 91, 109
links, 55–71
Nav-bars, 101–110
templates, 82–85, 91
Web pages, 10–11
Crop button, 27
cropping images, 27–28
CSS, 8, 22, 44
CSS Styles tab, 60–62, 104–105
.css suffix, 61, 62

D

Delimiter options, 46, 53
dependent files, 120, 122, 123
description, Web site, 112, 123
Description dialog box, 112
Design panel, 60, 94
Design view, 2, 8
digital camera software, xiii
Disconnect button, 117, 121, 122
Document toolbar, 2
Draw Layer button, 95, 96
Dreamweaver
    and image editing, 23, 35
    interface, 2–3
    purpose of, vii
    recommended book on, xiv, 22
Dreamweaver MX 2004: Visual QuickStart Guide, xiv, 22
Dreamweaver Site button, 4
.dwt suffix, 91

index

E

Edit button, Assets tab, 83, 89
Edit buttons, Property inspector, 24
Edit Font List option, 22
Edit icon, 78
Edit local copies... option, 6
Editable Region command, 84
editing
    images, 23, 35
    library items, 78–79
    tables, 48–49
    templates, 89–90
Email button, 64
Email Link dialog box, 64
email links, 64, 71
example files, xii
Expand/Collapse button, 116, 117, 118
Export Styles As CSS File dialog box, 61, 104
external links, 55, 58, 67, 71
external style sheets, 60–61, 91, 102, 105

F

favorites, 74–75
Favorites radio button, 75
File > New command, 10, 86
File > Save command, 11
file names, 22
file size, image, 24
files
    checking in/out, 8, 117, 123
    dependent, 120, 122, 123
    moving, 116
    uploading, 120–123
    viewing, 116
Files panel, 3, 111, 116–117
Files tab, 3, 11
Fireworks, xiii, 24
Folder icon, 6
Font menu, 12
fonts, 12, 22, 59

Format menu, 12, 16
Format Table dialog box, 50
formatting text, 13–14
FTP address, 7

G

Get button, 117
GIF images, 35
graphics. See images
graphics programs, 23
grid, 2, 38

H

H Space text box, 33, 35
Head button, 112
Header options, Table dialog, 39, 42, 53
headings, Web page, 16–17, 22
headlines, Web page, 39
home page, 9–22
    adding layers to, 94–96
    adding lists to, 18–19
    adding search terms to, 112–113
    adding text to, 12–15
    changing background for, 20–21
    creating, 10–11
    creating headings for, 16–17, 22
    creating Nav-bar for, 101–103. See also Nav-bar
    giving title to, 10, 11, 22
    naming, 10, 11, 22
    purpose of, 9
    saving, 11
    uploading to remote site, 120–121
horizontal rule, 35, 41, 76, 91
Horizontal Rule command, 41
hosting. See Web hosting
hot spots, 68–70, 72
.htm/.html suffix, 11
HTML, vii, 8, 22, 112, 123
hyperlinks, 55. See also links

I

image editors, xiii, 23
image maps, 24, 68–70, 72
images, 23–35
    adding space around, 33, 35
    adding to Nav-bar, 101–103
    adding to tables, 40–41, 53
    adding to Web pages, 25–26, 35
    adjusting brightness/contrast for, 29, 35
    aligning text with, 34
    background, 20
    creating alternate text for, 24, 26, 35
    creating links with, 67–70
    cropping, 27–28, 35
    duplicating, 30
    enlarging, 35
    marking as favorites, 74–75
    naming/renaming, 27
    reducing, 30–31, 35
    resampling, 31, 35
    saving, 26
    setting borders for, 24, 102
    sharpening, 31
    storing, 35
    tiled, 20
    viewing information about, 24, 35
    wrapping text around, 24, 32–33, 35
Images folder, 40
Import Tabular Data dialog box, 46
index file, 11, 22, 120
Insert > Image command, 40
Insert Table button, 39
Insert toolbar, 2, 25
internal links, 55, 56–57, 67, 71
internal style sheets, 60–61
Internet
    connecting to, 118–119
    publishing site on, 111
    uploading files to, 120–123
Invisible Elements command, 72

J

JPEG images, 35

K

keywords, 112, 123
Keywords dialog box, 112

L

labels, for table columns/rows,
    39, 42–43, 53
layers, 94–100
    adding to Web page, 94–96
    naming, 97
    pasting content into, 94
    positioning, 98–100, 110
    purpose of, 94
    selecting, 110
    setting height/width of, 99
    Web browser support for, 94
Layers tab, Design panel, 94
Layout toolbar, 39
.lbi suffix, 91
library items, 76–81
    and Basic Page column, 22
    creating, 76–77, 91, 109
    editing, 78–79
    file suffix for, 91
    inserting in Web page, 80–81
    naming, 77
    purpose of, 76
    saving Nav-bars as, 109
    and style sheets, 91
    yellow background for, 81
line breaks, 15, 101
link-related buttons, 55
links, 55–71
    changing color/style for,
        59–63, 71
    embedding email addresses
        in, 64, 71
    to items outside your own
        Web site, 58
    between pages on Web site,
        56–57, 108

purpose of, 55
testing, 57, 58, 70, 114–115
types of, 55
using images for, 67–70
within Web pages, 65–66
lists, 9, 18–19
Local Files pane, 120, 122
local site
    changing folder location
        for, 6
    entering FTP address for, 7
    naming/renaming, 5, 8
    setting up, 4–8
    uploading files to remote
        site from, 120–123
    viewing files on, 116–117
login name, 7, 8
logs folder, 123

M

Macintosh, text size on, 12, 22
Macromedia
    Dreamweaver MX 2004, vii–
        xiv. See also Dreamweaver
    Fireworks, 24
    Studio MX 2004, xiii
main.css style sheet, 62–63,
    102, 120
Map text window, 68
maps, image, 24, 68–70, 72

N

Named Anchor button, 65
naming
    editable regions, 84
    home pages, 10, 11, 22
    hot spots, 69
    images, 27
    layers, 97
    library items, 77
    local sites, 5, 8
    styles, 48, 104
    template-based pages, 87
    templates, 82

Nav-bar, 93–110
    adding images/text to,
        101–103
    adding layers to page for,
        94–96
    creating main, 101–103
    creating small version of,
        104–109
    eliminating borders in, 102
    positioning layers for,
        98–100
    purpose of, 93
    saving as library item, 109
    styling text in, 101–102,
        107, 108
navigation bar. See Nav-bar
New command, 10, 86
New Document dialog box, 10
New Editable Region dialog
    box, 84
New Folder command, 35
New from Template dialog
    box, 86
New Template button, 82
numbered lists, 18

O

Ordered List icon, 18
ordered lists, 18

P

padding, cell, 46
page-layout tools, 37, 94
Page Properties dialog box, 20
page titles, 10, 11, 22
paragraph breaks, 15, 32
paragraphs
    choosing font for, 12
    resizing text for, 14
    starting new, 13
passwords, 7, 8
PCs. See Windows systems
photos, 35. See also images
pixels, 14
Point to File icon, 56, 67, 69, 115

index

index

Properties command, 12
Property inspector, 3, 9
  correcting broken links
    with, 115
  image tools, 24
  opening, 12
  positioning layers with,
    98–100
  positioning Nav-bar content
    with, 102
publishing site, 111–123
  adding search terms,
    112–113
  checking links, 114–115
  connecting to Internet,
    118–119
  defined, 111
  uploading files, 120–123
Put button, 117, 120

R

Refresh button, 117, 121
remote site
  connecting to, 117, 118–119
  uploading files to, 120–123
  viewing files on, 116–117
Rename command, 27
Rename Style dialog box, 44
renaming items. See naming
Resample button, 31, 35
robot programs, 71
rollover links, 59
root folder, 26, 35
rule, horizontal, 76, 91
ruler, 2, 38

S

Save As dialog box, 11
saving
  home pages, 11
  images, 26
  Nav-bars, 109
  styles, 44
  templates, 85, 90, 91
scripts, 35

search engines, 112
search terms, 112–113, 123
Select Image Source dialog box,
  26, 40
Select Style Sheet File dialog
  box, 105
Sharpen button, 31
Sharpen slider, 31
Show Grid command, 38
Site Definition window, 6–8
Site radio button, 74
Size menu, 14
Snap To Grid command, 38
Sort Table dialog box, 51, 53
spacing, cell, 46
Split button, 113
Split view, 2
spreadsheet data, 46
Src box, Property inspector, 24
Standard button, 38
Standard toolbar, 2
Start Page, 22
Status dialog box, 119
Studio MX 2004, xiii
Style box, 13–14
Style drop-down menu, 48
style sheets, 22, 60–63, 91
styles
  naming, 48, 101, 104
  saving, 44
  for tables, 46–47, 53
  for text, 13–14, 101
subfolders, 35

T

tab-separated text, 46, 53
table-based Nav-bar, 104–108
Table dialog box, 39
table headers, 39, 42–43, 53
Table size options, Table dialog,
  39, 42
tables, 37–53
  adding images to, 40–41, 53
  adding to Web pages, 38–39
  applying colors to, 50, 53
  applying styles to, 44–45, 53

deleting cells in, 49
editing, 48–49
importing data into,
  46–47, 53
labeling columns/rows in, 39,
  42–43, 53
as page-layout tool, 37
selecting, 53
setting options for, 38–39
sorting, 51–52, 53
turning on grid/ruler for, 38
Tabular Data icon, 46
templates, 82–91
  adding content to, 83
  creating, 82–85, 91
  editing, 89–90
  file suffix for, 91
  generating pages based on,
    86–88
  marking editable regions in,
    84–85
  naming, 82
  opening, 83
  purpose of, 82
  replacing editable regions
    in, 88
  saving, 85, 90, 91
Templates tab, 86
Test Connection option, 7, 8
testing
  links, 57, 58, 70, 114–115
  online connection, 7, 8
text
  adding to Web page, 12–15
  applying styles to, 13–14
  choosing color for, 13
  choosing font for, 12
  linking to, 56–58, 108
  on Mac vs. Windows systems,
    12, 22
  sizing, 14, 22
  wrapping around images,
    24, 32–33, 35
Text Color box, 13
text styles, 22, 101
thumbnails, 30
tiled images, 20

timesavers, 73, 82
titles, page, 10, 11, 22
toolbars, 2
Towers, J. Tarin, xiv

U

Undo Crop command, 27
Unordered List icon, 19
uploading files, 120–123

V

V Space text box, 33, 35
VersionTracker, 23
views, 2, 8
visited links, 59, 71
visual handicaps,
    accommodating, 24, 35, 53
Visual QuickProject Guides, vii

W

Web browsers
    and Alt text, 24, 35
    checking remote site pages
      in, 121
    and layers, 94, 100
    and library items, 81
    and page titles, 11, 22

and table captions, 53
testing links in, 57–58, 64,
    70, 71
and visually impaired visitors,
    24, 35, 53
Web hosting, 7, 8
Web page. See also Web site
    adding images to, 25–26, 35
    adding layers to, 94–96
    adding lists to, 18–19
    adding tables to, 38–39
    adding title to, 10, 11, 22
    changing background for,
      20–21
    creating, 10–11
    creating headings for,
      16–17, 22
    creating links for, 55–71
    creating template for, 82–85.
      See also templates
    fixing mistakes in, 122
    updating, 122
    using tables to lay out, 37
Web publishing.
    See publishing site
Web search engines, 112
Web site
    adding navigation to, 93.
      See also Nav-bar
    adding search terms to,
      112–113

checking links in, 114–115
collaborating on, 8
creating home page for,
    10–11. See also home page
creating links for, 55–71. See
    also links
describing, 112, 123
inserting library items in,
    80–81
publishing, 111–123. See also
    publishing site
reusing items for, 73
setting up local version of,
    4–8. See also local site
this book's companion, xii
viewing files for, 3
Window > Properties
    command, 12
Windows systems, text size
    on, 12, 22
wrapping, text, 24, 32–33, 35

X

XML, 22

Y

yellow background, 81

Ready to Learn More?

If you enjoyed this project and are ready to learn more, pick up a *Visual QuickStart Guide*, the best-selling, most affordable, most trusted, quick-reference series for computing.

With more than 5.5 million copies in print, *Visual QuickStart Guides* are the industry's best-selling series of affordable, quick-reference guides. This series from Peachpit Press includes more than 200 titles covering the leading applications for digital photography and illustration, digital video and sound editing, Web design and development, business productivity, graphic design, operating systems, and more. Best of all, these books respect your time and intelligence. With tons of well-chosen illustrations and practical, labor-saving tips, they'll have you up to speed on new software fast.

> "*When you need to quickly learn to use a new application or new version of an application, you can't do better than the **Visual QuickStart Guides** from Peachpit Press.*"
>
> Jay Nelson
> *Design Tools Monthly*

www.peachpit.com